CASH COWS, PIGS AND JACKPOTS

CASH COWS, PIGS AND JACKPOTS

THE SIMPLEST PERSONAL FINANCE STRATEGY EVER

David Trahair, CA

John Wiley & Sons Canada, Ltd.

Library and Archives Canada Cataloguing in Publication Data

Trahair, David
   Cash cows, pigs and jackpots : the simplest personal finance strategy ever/ David Trahair.

Includes index.
Issued also in electronic formats.
ISBN 978-1-118-08351-2

   1. Finance, Personal.   I. Title.

HG179.T71 2012   332.024   C2012-902739-1

ISBN 978-1-118-08352-9 (eBk); 978-1-118-08353-6 (eBk); 978-1-118-08354-3 (eBk)

Production Credits
Cover design: Adrian So
Interior text design: Thomson Digital
Typesetter: Thomson Digital
Printer: Dickinson

John Wiley & Sons Canada, Ltd.
6045 Freemont Blvd.
Mississauga, Ontario
L5R 4J3

Printed in the United States
1 2 3 4 5 DPI 16 15 14 13 12

To Emily Yeskoo and her family.

Emily Yeskoo has a rare neurodegenerative disease that is terminal. At the age of 10 she was given three years to live. She is now 19, thanks to her fighting spirit and the loving support of her family: her mom Lindsey, dad Paul, brother Chris and sister Madeleine.

Emily is the inspiration for Toronto's first pediatric palliative care hospice called Emily's House. It will provide 24-hour care to terminally ill children so they don't have to face spending the rest of their lives in a hospital ward. It will be a place where they can learn, play, develop and grow...to be just kids, in a comfortable, child-friendly setting, with personalized family-centred programs.

It will also offer a welcome break to parents faced with the ultimate stress each and every day.

A portion of the proceeds from the sale of this book will go to Emily's House.

For more information please visit http://www.philipazizcentre.ca/ childrens-hospice.

CONTENTS

CONTENTS

Contents

CONTENTS

Contents

ACKNOWLEDGEMENTS

I could not have written this book if I had not been trained as a chartered accountant. In fact, finding the CA profession when I was a lost 23-year-old fresh out of university kind of saved me.

The CA profession has also recently given me the opportunity to teach and learn from other CAs. I give courses based on my books to CAs and other accountants in British Columbia, Alberta, Saskatchewan, Manitoba and Ontario. Through these courses I have met many incredible minds, some of whom have been instrumental in developing the content of this book.

First of all I have to thank Kurt Rosentreter, CA, CFP, CLU, TEP, FMA, CIMA, FCSI, CIM (no, I'm not kidding!). I first met Kurt taking one of the courses that he offers to CAs. I have never met anyone with his knowledge, qualifications and ability to explain complex financial issues in plain language. My conversations with him over the issues in this book and the examples he relayed were instrumental in making the book something that I hope you will find easy to understand and helpful in your own quest for solid financial footing. Kurt's website is www.kurtismycfo.com.

There are also many other CAs who have provided valuable advice, feedback and encouragement, including Ron Graham, Phil Goldband, Jeff Goldberg, Peter Poulimenakos, Peter Shennett and Brian Quinlan.

Acknowledgements

I also have the privilege of hearing from other people who aren't CAs but nonetheless teach me invaluable lessons. One such person is Debbie Spence, one of the best accountants I know. The other is Michel Boutin, who describes himself as a self-taught investor, but he is much more than that. He is also a wiz at Microsoft Excel, the complexities of Canadian income taxes, as well as fully bilingual. Thanks for all your feedback and contributions, Michel!

I would also like to thank all the great people at my publisher, John Wiley & Sons, for their hard work on this book, including Karen Milner, Lucas Wilk, Elizabeth McCurdy and Nicole Langlois. And thanks, of course, are due to my literary agent, Hilary McMahon, of Westwood Creative Artists.

Thanks also to two of my greatest backers, Gloria Krajacic and Michael Boyd, for their never ending support.

I would also like to thank my dad, Peter, for always being there when I needed him and for providing such a great example of how to live a happy, healthy, fulfilling life.

And of course to my kids. My buddy for life, my son, Kyle, and my angel, my daughter, Cassidy. You make life worth living!

Last but not least, the love of my life, my amazing wife, Elaine. Love forever.

INTRODUCTION

I have been researching and writing about personal financial issues for more than a decade now and have taught my theories to thousands of CAs over the last few years.

I have had lots of feedback and it has now become crystal clear to me:

Our quest to build wealth and secure a comfortable retirement often ends up making us poor and others rich.

Simply put, the accepted method of building wealth doesn't work anymore.

Think about it for a moment.

We are persuaded that the way to get wealthy is to build our assets and net worth, since that is the "true" measure of wealth. It's the measure of the value of what we own less the amounts that we owe. So we end up trying to build our assets—we load up on real estate, for instance, buying big houses and rental properties. Or we put money into the stock market, many of us using expensive mutual funds to do so.

And many of us use debt to do the building.

But you know what? The strategy is wrong. It's faulty logic that is sending many Canadians, and people around the world, on a journey to the poorhouse.

Why?

Because it ignores the one thing that overrides any strategy designed to build wealth.

It ignores the basic principle that has always existed.

It ignores the base logic that anyone who is truly rich knows.

It is this:

> **What we should really be focused on is not getting rich but plain old *cash flow*.**

Simple, isn't it? Yes, it is. It always has been and it always will be.

If you want to secure your financial future, forget all the fancy strategies like "leveraging" (borrowing to build wealth). Forget the fantasy that the stock market is going to make your financial dreams come true. Discard the notion that real estate is going to be the ride to wealth like it has been for past generations.

Forget those things because believing those concepts is likely to set you up for failure in the tough years that are coming.

CASH IS NOT KING

When I started laying the foundation for this book, I originally began with the old saying "Cash is king." But the more I thought about it, the more it didn't make sense. After all, with the extremely low interest rate environment we are in these days, sitting with cash is probably not the thing to do because it grows so slowly. Just look at what your bank savings account is paying—maybe 1%? Converting your assets to cash makes little sense as a result.

So what is "king" when it comes to personal finances? The answer is simple, and it's been the answer since money was invented. Here it is:

CASH FLOW IS KING

The more I think about it, the more I am convinced that cash flow really is king.

Aiming to build a million dollars in net assets sounds like a good plan—after all, that's how millionaire status is judged. The problem is that trying to get there often leaves people well short of the mark. One of the main reasons for this is that they bleed cash each and every day in their pursuit.

WHO GETS RICH OFF YOU

And who benefits from that? The people who know how to get rich by ensuring a cash flow gold mine for themselves—the investment companies that charge mutual fund fees, trailer fees, and commissions; the financial institutions that loan us the money to live the "lifestyle of our dreams" and then charge a huge amount of interest to service those debts; and the brokers who convince us to borrow to invest and "leverage" our way to riches.

IT'S NOT JUST THEM, IT'S US

But it's not just the financial institutions that feed the problem. In many cases, it's just our own logic that leads us astray. Take the idea of building wealth through acquiring real estate.

The truth is that buying too much real estate is often a sure-fire way to go broke because of the huge costs of acquiring and maintaining property. Simply buying too big a home to live in leaves many people poor—they simply can't afford the mortgage and the upkeep.

WANT TO GET RICH QUICK?

This book was written to get you back to the basics. It was written to shine a light on why the current method of building wealth is a mirage, a trick designed to make others rich while sentencing the rest of us to a lifetime of constantly trying to get ahead, of aiming for the brass ring of financial freedom ... and never reaching it.

If you still believe that you can get rich easily, quickly, automatically or even instantly, I can't help you. Put this book down and pretend it does not exist. There are plenty of other books out there that make promises like that. Many of them sell millions of copies. Well, at least someone is getting rich.

If you are one of the many people who will buy anything that promises to reveal the secret to getting rich easily, this is not the book for you.

I just picked up such a book that promises quick and easy riches. It's a very short, simple book—only 120 pages—but the premise when you actually read it is just silly. To get rich all you have to do is set a definitive goal for the amount of money you will make in a certain number of years and it will happen. C'mon.

Well, the introduction says it has been published in 30 editions all over the world and sold more than a million copies.

And that is the problem—millions of people still believe there is a trick to getting rich and many put their financial lives at risk trying to find the secret.

BACK TO BASICS

I hate to bring you back to earth but there is no secret to riches and, the sooner you realize that, the sooner you will be on the path to true financial freedom.

That is what this book is about—it's the plain truth about what is really important and exactly how to secure your financial future. Oh, and it is so simple you should be able to explain it to your kids.

Here it is.

THE CASH COW
STRATEGY

It's very, very simple. From now on, before you spend any more money on anything, before you jump into an investment opportunity, before you sign a deal for a new car or a new house or condo, before you put another cent on your credit card, before you borrow another dime, stop for a moment and consider the cash flow implications of the thing. Ask yourself these questions:

- Is this a cash cow?
- Is this a cash pig?
- Is there a potential jackpot later on?

If you do this from now on, you will transform your personal finances. You just might find that you'll significantly decrease your stress level as well. If you embrace this concept, it has the power to change your life for the better. I know because it changed mine.

Let me explain.

CASH COWS

If you look up the definition at www.investopedia.com here is what you'll see:

A business, product or asset that, once acquired and paid off, will produce consistent cash flow over its lifespan. This term is a metaphor for a dairy cow that produces milk over the course of its life and requires little maintenance. A dairy cow is an example of a cash cow, as after the initial capital outlay has been paid off, the animal continues to produce milk for many years to come.

That would be a good thing to have, agreed?

Think about the things in your life that provide cash for you on a consistent basis.

What do you think your biggest cash cow is going to be? Your job? Maybe your RRSP? Perhaps your investments? What about a rental property? Maybe you're lucky enough to have a guaranteed defined benefit pension plan—will that be your best cash cow? What about your small business if you are self-employed?

Your answer is so important I'm going to ask you to put this book down, close your eyes and give it some thought. What is the thing in your life that is going to bring in the most amount of cash over your lifetime?

Don't rush this. The more you understand what we are about to discuss, the better off you'll be.

Pull out a piece of paper and a pen. If you have a notebook or an iPad, start your word processor, and write or type the following:

The thing in my life that will bring in the most cash in my lifetime is:

_____

Because I want to give you the benefit of finding out a bit about how you think and how you prioritize things, I'm not going to reveal it to you here. You'll have to wait until the next chapter. Resist the urge to look ahead—it won't be long.

CASH PIGS

A cash pig is the opposite of a cash cow. It is something that constantly drains cash from your pocket. That doesn't mean it's a bad thing. Many cash pigs are useful, sometimes vital, things that many of us can't do without. Can you think of one?

How about a car?

A car is a cash pig no matter whether you buy or lease. It serves a vital function—getting us to work, for instance—but there is no doubt it is a cash pig. It requires cash to buy it whether we pay with a cheque, take out a loan or lease it. There are also all the annual operating costs such as gas and oil, insurance, licensing, repairs and maintenance, etc.

For most of us, the fixed and operating costs add up to thousands of dollars a year. Again, that doesn't necessarily make them bad; it just means they eat up a lot of cash. And of course some of them are bigger pigs than others.

The purpose of identifying things that are cash pigs is not so we can avoid them at all costs. The purpose is to realize how much cash they will cost us so we can make sure we choose one that we can afford and not one that would bleed our bank account dry.

CASH JACKPOTS

Winning the lottery is the most obvious example of a cash jackpot. No doubt about it—in fact, winning millions of dollars or more (tax-free) would be the definition of a jackpot.

But the odds are very long.

The key point to realize is that cash jackpots are rarely guaranteed. They are usually just potential jackpots. But potential jackpots come with a big risk—the risk that the jackpot may not happen at all.

Betting your future finances on a potential jackpot is like playing with dynamite. Don't do it.

But it seems to me that many people spend a vast amount of time (and sometimes money) hoping for a jackpot. The problem is that this opens them up to being ripped off. In *Enough Bull* I talked about simply avoiding any situation that could result in personal financial disaster if it went wrong. I talked about Ponzi schemes.

A Ponzi scheme takes advantage of people who are hoping for a jackpot. It is a scam where the perpetrator convinces people to give them money and in return they'll usually be offered a "guaranteed" high rate of return on their money. In reality the schemer just spends all the money, usually on a lavish lifestyle. The "guarantee" is a lie. There is no such thing as a guaranteed high rate of return.

I now see stories of the latest Ponzi scheme nearly every month. In fact, there were two stories of major Ponzi schemes within 10 days recently in the Toronto newspapers. The dollars lost are staggering—one of the schemes saw $129 million evaporate.

THIS IS NOT A PHILOSOPHY; IT'S ABOUT CASH FLOW

Keep in mind as you read further that we are thinking about the cash flow implications of things so we can make better financial decisions. We are not making a determination about the value or worth of the things.

In other words, we are not making a judgement that cows are good and pigs are bad.

It is also not a philosophical statement about whether things that have the potential for a jackpot are to be avoided. Some jackpots are good and some are not.

It is simply to get you to think about how each decision you make is going to affect what goes in and out of your bank account on a daily, weekly and monthly basis. Note that "cash flow" does not mean just actual cash, it includes all methods of receiving and paying money. That includes actual cash you receive, but also electronic deposits such as your paycheque as well as money transfers from others. Cash you pay out can be in the form of actual cash withdrawals from your account as well as cheques you write and electronic payments and transfers out to pay bills, etc. And of course anything you buy using a credit card, even though it does not have to paid back until later, is outgoing money that affects your cash flow.

Cows and Pigs Can Change

This is also not a permanent branding procedure. Things can, and often do, change characteristics over their lives. A cash pig may become a cash cow later on.

RRSPs would be a good example. As we work and put money into them, they take cash out of our bank accounts, even after you factor in the temporary tax refund you receive for the contributions. They are cash pigs as we make contributions to them.

The payoff comes after we retire. When we start drawing money out of them, they fit the definition of a cash cow. Obviously just how good a cow they are depends on how well our investment strategy worked over the years.

One Person's Pig May Be Another Person's Cow

In some cases the same thing may be a cash pig to one person and a cash cow to another.

Take a gold credit card with a balance owing, for example. The customer pays interest at over 20% on any balance he can't pay off. The bank collects that interest every month. For the customer in this arrangement, that credit card is a cash pig. For the card issuer, it's a cash cow.

Which side would you rather be on?

CASH COW, PIG OR JACKPOT?

There are hundreds of things that we come across in our lives that significantly affect our cash flow. In most cases it is tough to put one label on a thing.

Some cost a lot of money up front, and continue to demand cash year after year to maintain, but they provide the potential for a large windfall gain at the end. That would be a cash pig with a potential jackpot. The house you are likely sitting in comes to mind.

Other items may cost very little up front and provide a jackpot of cash at the end. A penny stock that actually does take off and sells for 1,000 times what you paid is arguably neither a cash cow nor a pig. It's a low-cost bet that pays off—a jackpot.

A cash pig may serve a useful purpose, or it may not. A smoking habit fits the bill as a cash pig without benefits. There is also no hope for a jackpot for a smoker, just years and years of cash drain (and, of course, probably much pain and suffering).

Let's discuss a number of common things.

A House or Condo

What about the biggest asset that most of us will ever own—our house or condo? Well, I have owned three different houses and I can tell you a house is a cash pig.

Again, that doesn't make it bad. In fact, I would argue that a reasonable house that we can afford is one of the best investments we can make. But a home is costly from a cash flow point of view. That is because, just like a car, there is the cash required to buy it (the down payment and closing costs) plus all the ongoing costs such as mortgage payments (including interest), property taxes, insurance, heating and electricity, repairs and maintenance, etc.

While there is little doubt that a house or condo is a cash pig in the years that we are living in it, it has the potential to become a jackpot if we sell it at the right time for more than we paid for it. There is even an added benefit: for principal residences (the one we live in) in Canada, any capital gains are tax-free.

But if you are new to the housing market, you've got to think of the odds of housing profits in the future versus the past before you buy.

Over the last 50 years many people were lucky enough to realize huge gains on the sale of their houses. For example, I know of some houses that were purchased for under $50,000 in the 1960s that are now worth a million dollars. Houses such as this have risen in value by 20 times in 50 years. That's an annual return of 6.2% per year and there is no tax on the eventual sale, assuming it's your principal residence. To make that kind of rate of return in the stock market you'd have to earn 10% or more per year before taxes—extremely unlikely, especially these days.

When we look into the future and consider the demographics of an aging population, it is difficult to visualize growth like that going forward.

Look at it this way: Decades ago, people typically bought houses that were two to three times their annual household income. For example, a family that earned $50,000 would buy a house for $100,000 to $150,000. Now it seems many are willing to commit to buying a house that costs 10 or more times their income. That is not a good idea. Just because prices are rising at incredible rates and banks seem willing to lend excessive amounts of money does not mean you can afford it.

I don't know about you, but thinking about a million dollar house selling for $20 million kind of blows me away. Think of the salary you'll need to afford that. My gut feeling is that the housing jackpots are going to be a lot smaller going forward.

Gambling

While most lottery tickets have a low up-front cost and no ongoing costs that define a cash pig, as I have said, they have only a potential jackpot at the end. The ticket becomes a jackpot if it wins, and an entertainment expense if it doesn't.

But what about those unfortunate souls who get addicted to gambling and can't stay out of the casinos or away from the on-line gambling sites? To them, the habit is not an entertainment expense. Even if they win the odd time, the deck is stacked against them. For some, their habit becomes the biggest cash pig they'll ever have to deal with. Many end up facing financial ruin.

Of course, to the casino, gambling is a cash cow. They can't lose, even if you do. That's because they retain a significant amount of the money contributed. I'd rather own part of a casino than gamble in one.

Personal Debt

Personal debt is a cash pig. For some people, depending on how much of it they have and the interest rate, it can be an absolute cash hog.

But it's interesting to note that a lot depends on what's on the other side of the equation. What was the debt used for? If it was used to buy a reasonable house in which you live, the debt is associated with an asset that you can enjoy, and it may even rise in value and provide a jackpot later on.

If it's consumer debt, such as credit cards and lines of credit that were used to pay for trips and toys you can't really afford, it is a cash pig with no redeeming qualities. The staggering amount of consumer debt outstanding today in Canada is a major risk to the financial stability of our country. Anyone who has excessive levels of consumer debt will tell you it is a cash pig—a cash pig with the potential to bankrupt a person if it can't be paid back.

When it comes to debt it is important to note that corporations are much different than individuals. Most corporations operate under the "going concern" assumption that they will go on forever and never have to repay all their debts. They are, therefore, dependent on the financial institutions continuing to lend them money. But if they are big enough, they have power. The banks can't simply say: "Pay it all back now." If they did, most companies would state the obvious: "If you call our loan, that will put us out of business and you'll get nothing." Or, more likely, they'll just take their loan business to another financial institution.

We as individuals don't have the power that corporations do. We can only get out of debt with plain old hard work to either increase our incomes or reduce our expenses, or ideally both. Of course we may get lucky and win a jackpot and be able to get debt-free that way, but that is one risky strategy that may work for one in a million.

So we see that many things have two sides we need to consider. That's just like basic double entry bookkeeping. Every transaction is not a debit or a credit. Each transaction is both a debit and a credit.

Used wisely, personal debt can and does work. It can bring us the things we want and need. But if it is used to fuel an over-spending lifestyle or take a huge risk on an investment that might (or might not) rise in value, it can be a real financial hog. That hog can, and just might, roll over and crush you.

Defined Benefit (DB) Pension Plans

This is an interesting one. Most people think of a DB plan as a cash cow. But it really depends on the situation.

Basically they work something like this: you work for a company or government for, say, 35 years and you earn 2% of your salary for each year you work—so you are guaranteed 70% of your final year's salary (often the average of your last three to five years) from the year you retire until the year you die. In some cases the amounts are even adjusted for inflation and there may be a survivor benefit so your remaining spouse still gets a percentage of what you used to get— often around 60% or so. Under the typical DB plan, you can't run out of money.

But some plans are funded, to a large degree, by the employer. The employees make little, if any, contribution during their working years. This is the type of plan everyone would like to have—low or no contributions and guaranteed cash for life after you retire. That is a cash cow.

In most cases, however, the employees also have to contribute to the DB plan. One popular plan I looked at recently requires matching contributions—the employer and the employee pay the same amount into it each year. For 2012 the contribution rate for members who plan to retire at 65 was 8.3% for earnings up to the CPP earnings limit of $50,100 and 12.8% for earnings higher than that. That means a plan member earning $100,000 in 2012 would have to pay $10,545 into his or her pension plan—more than 10% of gross pay. Even though the contributions are tax-deductible, that is a lot of money. This plan is a cash pig during the employment years, and a cash cow after retirement.

The lucky people who have DB plans never had to worry about what was in the plan. Those who are trying to fund their retirement with an RRSP do have to worry since there is no guarantee—you could run out before you die if the amount in your RRSP and its future growth are not large enough to meet your spending needs.

That is the problem with RRSPs. They are a defined amount at a point in time—your retirement date. Whether they will be a big enough cash cow for you after that time will depend on how much the investments grow each year versus how much you need to take out each year to feed your cash pigs.

With a DB plan there is no such worry, since the employer is guaranteeing your payments for the rest of your life. Even if you live to 100, you will still get your guaranteed cash each and every month until you leave the earth, unless the company goes bankrupt.

At least that's how they are supposed to work.

The problem is that due to the ultra-low interest rates and the poor stock market returns of the last few years, the entities that do need to worry about what the DB pension plan assets are (that is, the company or government that has to pay out the pensions) are having a tough time growing the assets to a large enough amount to be able to pay the promised pensions.

Many plans are significantly under-funded as a result and this is a major problem for most plan administrators and their members.

Canada Pension Plan and Old Age Security

The government pension plans pose an interesting challenge. As Canadians, whether we are employed or self-employed, we are required to pay premiums to the Canada Pension Plan (CPP). In return, we are provided a pension when we retire—usually from age 65, but sometimes as early as age 60. Is the CPP a cash pig or a cash cow?

You'll find people who argue both sides. I've talked to dozens of them. The answer is that it depends on your circumstances. In other words, how many years you paid into it and how many years you live to receive money out of it. To answer the question, Chapter Eight will detail all the new rules on CPP that are now coming into play. We'll also look at a spreadsheet that you can download for free from my website that will calculate the internal rate of return of your CPP under various assumptions to determine if it's a good investment.

The federal government also just proposed rule changes for the Old Age Security (OAS) pension in the budget of March 29, 2012. The full details will be discussed in Chapter Nine. But what is OAS—a cash cow or a cash pig? Well, since we don't pay into the OAS like we do the CPP (it is paid out of current government revenue and therefore affects the annual deficit, unlike the CPP, which doesn't), it is a cash cow for those of us who receive it. And of course it is a cash pig to the federal government, which has to pay it.

Kids

Parents, like me, realize that our kids are by far the most important things that will ever enter our lives. They transcend money. They provide meaning to our lives.

In fact, I have never met an accountant who did a Net Present Value of the future cash flows calculation before deciding to have a kid!

But let's face it, they cost money to raise. Am I right?

What does that make them?

Well, from a purely unemotional point of view, they are, well, um...

They are cash...

Let's settle on "cash piglets," okay?

This book is not designed to help you decide how many kids to have. That is your decision. But seriously, we need to think about what we are spending our money on and how it affects us as well as them. Do they get everything they want whenever they want it? I know it's difficult to resist giving them all the things and experiences we perhaps never had as kids. But what is that teaching them? To expect Mom and Dad to give them whatever they feel the need for at the drop of a hat?

That would seem to be a bad idea from a kid-raising point of view, and secondarily from a cash flow point of view.

Anyway, I'm not trying to give you a sermon here. I'm trying to get you to think about your priorities, giving consideration to the cash flow effects.

A BIGGER VIEW: GOVERNMENT DEBT

Many governments have been incurring deficits (spending more than they bring in each year) and running up debts like never before. Canada is no exception.

The people running the federal government have to deal with a cash pig. The amount of cash required each year to run the federal government is staggering. The annual deficit, or loss, for the year ended March 31, 2011, was $33.4 billion. That is $91.5 million every day, including weekends.

But they have options that we don't as individuals. They have the power to raise taxes. This would seem to be a good way out of debt. But how often do politicians actually do that? Obviously it's unpopular and therefore politicians usually resist doing it until there is no alternative to help balance the budget.

There is also the issue of the connection between raising taxes and the economy. Besides individual voter revolt, there is the effect of increased taxes on corporate profits. Maybe some of the country's most profitable companies might decide to move operations to another country with lower corporate tax rates, taking thousands of jobs and millions in corporate taxes with them.

So the governments tend to continue on the treadmill of not raising taxes, and spending more than they bring in. Who pays for the increasing debt loads? Future generations. They will most likely be saddled with huge amounts of taxes they'll have to pay to avoid future government bankruptcy.

Don't get me started on the subject of debt. I could write a whole book on it. Actually, I already did. It's called *Crushing Debt*.

WHY DON'T PEOPLE FOLLOW THIS BASIC STRATEGY?

So why don't people live their lives focusing on the simple strategy of managing plain old cash flow? Because many of them are looking for an easier way. Many believe that their money problems would disappear if they just were able to find that one investment that would guarantee them a 10% return. Or if they won the lottery they'd be living on Easy Street.

Anything but having to slog away at the office or the warehouse day after day.

Many people are hoping for the day when they will be rich enough to quit work and "retire." They'll try almost anything, even trusting a stranger who promises to make them wealthy.

For most of them, this doesn't work. They never reach their goal. And even for the ones that do, even if they qualify as millionaires, they find out that it's not the answer.

The rest of this book is devoted to getting you to focus on what is important, so you can enjoy your life. It is the better way.

TAKING CARE OF YOUR BIGGEST CASH COW

If you had something that gave you money on a consistent basis day-after-day, year-after-year, you'd probably take care of it, right? You'd want to protect it so that the cash would keep coming, wouldn't you?

In the last chapter I asked you to spend some time thinking about what your most important cash cow was. What was your answer?

Your job?

Your house?

Borrowing to invest in the stock market?

Winning the lottery?

A huge inheritance?

For the vast majority of us, those answers are all wrong.

YOUR BIGGEST CASH COW IS...

You.

That's right. For most of us, the greatest source of cash, by far, is our ability to work and earn income. That may sound obvious now but many people will not have written "Me" on that line.

Think about your own situation. Where does your cash come from? For most of us, it's our job or self-employment earnings.

I know this because I am an accountant and have seen thousands of personal income tax returns of Canadians, from low earners to multi-millionaires. All you have to do is look at the first page of their T1 General income tax return. Usually the amount of income from employment or self-employment dwarfs the amount of income from other sources, like investment or rental income, during the working years. And let's be clear, your working years are the most important years when it comes to your personal finances. How you handle your life and money during this time is what will determine how well you can retire.

Of course it is possible that a large source of cash may not be taxable and therefore not show up on your tax return (the proceeds on the sale of your principal residence, for example), but that is a potential windfall gain that may or may not happen. We've already discussed potential jackpots such as this—they may happen, but they may not. Would you bet everything on the chance that it might? I wouldn't recommend it.

Drilling down a bit deeper into cash flow, we need to be clear that there is a big difference between income and cash flow. For example, we may earn, say, $80,000 from our job—that's our gross pay that goes on page one of our income tax return—but it's not our take-home pay, which is the actual spendable cash we get.

In fact, I just entered $80,000 in gross pay for a person living in British Columbia in 2012 and after federal and provincial income tax, CPP and EI, the take-home pay is $59,885. That clearly illustrates the difference between income and cash—$20,115 in this case.

The same goes for investment income. Unless our investments are in a Tax-Free Savings Account (TFSA), taxes take away cash, depending on the type of income and tax bracket.

So taxes are obviously a vital factor in the Cash Cow Strategy.

But let's get back to the most important cash cow—you.

If you are the greatest source of cash, it makes sense to focus on growing, preserving and protecting your ability to earn money, right? Let's explore this a bit.

Perhaps you spent thousands of dollars on your university degree. Why did you do that? To increase your knowledge, of course, but also because you were hoping to find a job or career that pays you more than if you did not have a degree. But even if you have the education and can find a job in your field, you need the engine to use it. That engine is you—your physical and mental being, your brain and muscle power.

You need to work on maintaining your physical and mental capacities on a daily basis or the engine may slow down and even stop working some day. Even if it doesn't stop, if you let yourself get run down physically or emotionally, you are not going to operate at peak capacity.

HOW TO PROTECT YOUR BIGGEST CASH COW

Most people spend more time deciding what to wear than they do maintaining their health. That is nuts.

I'd like you to indulge yourself for a few minutes. I am going to make the case that looking after yourself is not selfish. In fact, it is the most important thing you should do and yet many people simply don't do it.

We all know what we should do to look after ourselves but many of us don't act on our knowledge. We know that to keep healthy we need to eat well-balanced meals, get regular exercise and plenty of sleep.

This becomes more important as we age. Remember the days when you were in your twenties and you could go out and have five drinks, party until 2:00 a.m. on a weeknight, grab a few hours' sleep and then head into work for a full day? I can tell you from personal experience that trying this in your early fifties is not a good idea.

No matter what age you are, I recommend that you start trying to take better care of yourself.

Is Your Body Trying to Tell You Something?

In my own case I never used to worry too much about my health. I haven't really had to watch my weight and have been fortunate enough not to have too many health-related issues. I do, however, suffer from ophthalmic migraines, commonly referred to as migraine aura without headache, and have since I was a kid. In my case the symptoms usually involve temporary visual disturbances lasting for about 20 minutes that I can best describe as starting with a small blank spot in my vision followed by a jagged multi-coloured zigzag arch that changes shape before it disappears.

Since they are usually painless, they are more of a distraction than anything else and so for a long time I just put up with them.

For whatever reason, over the past few years since I turned 50, the symptoms expanded and became more frequent, so I went to see my doctor.

He sent me to a wonderful headache specialist. She sent me for all the tests to rule out the bad stuff—eye test, blood work, an MRI (good news: there is "nothing" in my head, at least that's good news when you're talking to a headache specialist) and a sleep study. She also recommended that I start taking a vitamin B supplement (B100) and 300 to 500 mg of magnesium glycinate every day. Turns out I have some problem retaining magnesium.

I was also told to stop drinking coffee and try ginger tea. In addition, the doctor recommended I make sure I get regular exercise, maybe even try yoga, read up on meditation techniques and monitor my diet.

I started integrating her recommendations into my life the next day.

What about you? Is anything bothering you health-wise that you maybe should have checked out? Even if you feel fine, why not start taking care of yourself before your body gives you the signals?

Let's start with your diet.

WARNING: I am not a doctor so don't base your medical decisions on the following words—consult a medical specialist first.

Are You Eating Well?

It's so common to hear that we should eat a well-balanced diet that most of us tune out the advice. "Yeah, yeah, I know...whatever," we say. Ever heard of the Canada Food Guide? It's that thing that lists what the average Canadian should eat every day. The myth is that it is difficult to follow—how can you possibly eat seven servings of vegetables every day, for example?

Well, have you actually ever looked at it? I hadn't either.

But we're going to look at it now. Just Google "Canada's Food Guide" and you'll come to Health Canada's home page on food and nutrition.[1] The guide is available in English and French and nine additional languages. The site is very well laid out and easy to navigate.

---

[1] http://www.hc-sc.gc.ca/fn-an/food-guide-aliment/index-eng.php

The following is the Food Guide chart that shows how much you need from each of the four food groups every day:[2]

Canada's Food Guide How Much Food You Need Every Day	Children			Teens		Adults			
	2–3	4–8	9–13	14–18		19–50		51+	
	Girls & Boys			F	M	F	M	F	M
Vegetables and Fruit	4	5	6	7	8	7–8	8–10	7	7
Grain Products	3	4	6	6	7	6–7	8	6	7
Milk and Alternatives	2	2	3–4	3–4	3–4	2	2	3	3
Meat and Alternatives	1	1	1–2	2	3	2	3	2	3

Aha! Here is where the myth that you'll need seven servings of vegetables a day comes from. It's actually vegetables *or* fruit.

Why not print out this chart and put it on your fridge to remind the family what they should aim for?

For Those Who Are Too Busy

Now I know for a fact that the majority of people that read the past few paragraphs aren't going to do anything about it. "Life is too busy to take the time to look at tables and track food quantities," they might say. I hope that doesn't describe you, but if it does, Health Canada suggests you simply try to do the following:

- Eat one dark green and one orange vegetable a day.
- Choose vegetables and fruit prepared with little or no added fat, sugar or salt.
- Choose grain products that are lower in fat, sugar or salt.
- Drink skim, 1% or 2% milk each day, or substitute soy beverage instead of milk.

---

[2] http://www.hc-sc.gc.ca/fn-an/food-guide-aliment/basics-base/quantit-eng.php

- Have meat alternatives such as bean, lentils and tofu often.
- Eat at least two servings of fish each week.
- Select lean meat and alternatives prepared with little or no added fat or salt.
- Satisfy your thirst with water.

The key to it all is to begin at the grocery store. Take this list with you to make sure you and your family have the healthy food options available to you when you eat.

Let's move on to exercise.

How Much Exercise Do You Get?

Canada's Food Guide also addresses physical activity. It recommends that adults aim for 2.5 hours of moderate to vigorous physical activity every week and that children and youth engage in at least an hour a day of physical activity.

For us adults, that is not a lot of time in a week. Look at it this way: there are 168 hours in a week, so 2.5 hours is only 1.5% of the time. Surely you can make time for that.

Personally I find a Stairmaster in the basement perfect. I don't have to join an expensive gym. I don't ever have to worry about the weather and I can listen to my favourite music as I exercise. I generally go for 30 minutes five times a week. If I miss a few days I can feel it—the stress builds up and reminds me to get back to it.

How Much Sleep Do You Get?

When I searched the Internet for "recommended sleep per night," the general consensus seems to be that the average adult needs approximately seven hours of sleep per night. Children and teenagers need even more—about nine to 10 hours each night (so that's why one of my teenagers is still in bed at 2:00 p.m. as I write this!).

Without adequate sleep you are more susceptible to health problems such as heart disease, obesity, stroke, diabetes and depression.

In an excellent article by CBC News dated December 2, 2010,[3] the results of a sleep poll conducted by Leger Marketing for CBC News found

---

[3] http://www.cbc.ca/news/health/story/2010/12/02/f-sleep-tips.html

that "6 out of 10 Canadians get about an hour less than the 6-8 hours of sleep a night experts say most adults need to feel refreshed and to perform optimally throughout the day."

Nearly 58% of Canadians polled said they often feel tired. About a third said they don't have enough time, another 32% said they regularly wake up and can't get back to sleep and a further 27% said they have too much on their mind to relax.

How to Get a Good Night's Sleep

The CBC article has an excellent checklist summarizing how to get a good night's sleep:[4]

- Keep a regular schedule.
- Eat a healthy diet and get regular exercise.
- Avoid napping during the day.
- Avoid caffeine, nicotine and alcohol.
- Relax and unwind before sleep.
- Make sure your room is conducive to sleep.
- If your mattress is old, consider buying a new one.
- Make sure your stomach is not too empty or full before going to bed.
- Get out of bed if you can't sleep.
- If your thoughts are keeping you awake, get up and write them down.

THE VALUE OF HARD WORK

Obviously it makes sense to work at building our skill sets with personal and professional development, but if you are really interested in making more money, consider making yourself stand out from the crowd. It seems to me that individuals who go beyond what is asked of them are rare. If you make yourself one of the few, you'll probably have much greater success finding and keeping active employment and making more money.

This is especially true for the youth of today. Finding and competing for jobs going forward is getting tougher by the day. If you

---

[4] Sources: National Sleep Foundation, The College of Family Physicians of Canada, Canadian Health Network

are a hard worker, word of mouth will go a long way to ensuring you work.

Let me tell you a story about that. I'll call it "One Dirty Window."

We get the exterior windows on our house cleaned every year or so by a window cleaning service. Since we've been living there for about a decade, that's 10 times. In all those years, there has been one small basement double-paned window that has remained dirty because it is at ground level. It's the one I look out of every time I use my Stairmaster to exercise, and in all those years, it has never been cleaned. That is because there is a screen that needs to be removed from the outside by pulling a couple of knobs. None had bothered to do that even though the dirt was clearly on the outside.

After our most recent cleaning, I was on the Stairmaster exercising when I noticed something strange. I could see a part of my neighbour's house that I hadn't noticed before. The window had been cleaned spotless!

The new cleaning company, College Pro, had done what no other service had done. The college students on the crew had gone the extra mile and did a great job. It may not sound like a big thing but making that extra effort has made me a client for life and likely to recommend them to my friends and neighbours. That's the benefit of hard work—your reputation will put you in good stead for future work.

SUMMING UP HEALTHY LIVING

It just makes sense to treat ourselves well—eat healthy and get plenty of exercise and sleep. Think of the time and effort you put into this as the best investment you'll ever make. You'll enable yourself to work more efficiently for longer, and that will mean more cash. The added benefit of this focus goes beyond simple money, of course—life is more enjoyable if we are well rested, well nourished and engaged in activities that we enjoy.

Another major benefit will be your health level during your retirement years. If you treat yourself well during your active, pre-retirement years, you are more likely to be healthier during your retirement years. And that means fewer health problems that can be very costly.

Keep active, fit and healthy. The alternative may lead to a depressing retirement filled with costs you don't need. Don't set yourself up to be your worst cash pig after your working days are done.

WHO WANTS TO BE
A MILLIONAIRE?

This chapter is going to explore the complicated relationship between money and happiness. After all, what good is money without happiness?

Many people live their lives dreaming of becoming a millionaire. People with that much money must be happy, right? Let's find out whether that is true.

WHAT IS "RICH"?

The common measurement of "rich" is net worth. It's pretty simple to calculate. All you do is list all the things you own (house, car, RRSPs, investments, rental properties, etc.) and the market value of each. Then you list the current balance of your debts (mortgage, car loan, credit card balances, lines of credit, etc.). Subtract total debts from total assets and there you go—the difference is your net worth.

A millionaire is usually defined as someone who has a net worth of $1 million or more.

Net Worth Is a Lousy Measure of Wealth

But there is a problem. In fact, there are a few problems with this measure.

Mixing Pre-Tax and After-Tax Amounts

First of all, net worth statements mix apples and oranges and can therefore be very misleading. Let's look at a simple example.

Would you rather be family #1 or family #2?

	Family #1	Family #2
Assets		
Principal residence	$300,000	$300,000
RRSP (making 4% per year)	$200,000	$0
Total assets	$500,000	$300,000
Debts		
Mortgage (at 4% per year)	($200,000)	$0
Net worth	$300,000	$300,000

On the face of it you would be indifferent, right? Wrong.

That's because the measure of net worth in this case ignores one huge thing: income taxes.

If you were to cash in both families' assets, the RRSP would be taxed upon withdrawal. In Ontario today the top marginal income tax rate is 46%. If the $200,000 was withdrawn in one year by someone in the top tax bracket, $92,000 would go to the tax department and only $108,000 would be left. That would not be enough to pay off the mortgage and would leave net worth for family #1 at only $208,000 versus $300,000 for family #2.

Ignores Cash Flow

But there is more to the story that is key to the Cash Cow Strategy. We need to look at the cash flow history of both families both before—and after—this snapshot of a point in time.

Let's look back over the 10 years prior to this net worth statement.

The members of family #1 made RRSP contributions of $16,659 per year for 10 years. Simply put, the future value of $16,659 per year for 10 years growing at an annual compound rate of 4% would grow to $200,000.

Assuming the RRSP contributors in family #1 had been in the top marginal tax bracket of 46%, they would have received annual tax refunds of $7,663 (46% of $16,659) so their net annual cash outflows were $8,996 ($16,659 less $7,663). That's a total cash outflow of $89,960 over the 10 years.

Family #2 did not make any RRSP contributions. Instead, they have paid off the $200,000 mortgage. That required monthly payments of $2,022, or $24,264 annually. That is $242,640 over the 10 years versus only $89,960 for RRSP family #1.

But here is the thing that many people forget. Family #1 had $200,000 in mortgage debt for the entire 10 years. Since that mortgage was not being paid down (an interest-only mortgage like the Manulife One account) they had to pay $8,000 per year in interest. That's $80,000 in interest over the 10 years.

The cash flow scorecard is therefore:

Annual Cash Out		
	Family #1	**Family #2**
RRSP contributions	$16,659	$0
RRSP refund	($7,663)	$0
Net RRSP contributions	$8,996	$0
Mortgage payments	$8,000	$24,264
Total annual cash out	$16,996	$24,264
Total 10-year cash out	$169,960	$242,640

Getting back to the net worth analysis, we saw that, after adjusting for taxes on the RRSP, family #2 would be better off than family #1 by $92,000.

The main reason for this is that family #2 didn't get any RRSP refund but instead paid a similar amount as family #1 and used the full amount to pay down the mortgage. In other words, family #1 paid $24,659 per year (RRSP of $16,659 and interest of $8,000) whereas family #2 paid $24,264 per year. That's a small annual difference of

$395 meaning that, excluding the RRSP refund, family #2 paid $3,950 less than family #1 over the 10 years.

But family #1 was receiving RRSP refunds of $7,663 per year and simply spent that money. That was a total of $76,630 over the 10 years. The total 10-year difference in total cash outflow in the chart above is $72,680 ($242,640 − $169,960).

The difference is family #1's RRSP refunds of $76,630 less the annual difference of $3,950 (10 times the $395). That equals $72,680.

There is no magic here, but we need to dig a little deeper.

In our after-tax net worth analysis we have assumed that family #1 cashes in its RRSP when in reality they probably would not. Instead, they might leave the funds in to compound on a tax-deferred basis for future cash inflows that will be taxed. Of course this whole analysis assumes the RRSP investments make 4%, which they may not.

But we must also consider one other vital point about family #1's future cash flow.

Family #1 now has to pay the $242,640 over the next 10 years to pay off their mortgage. Family #2 doesn't. They can instead use that money for whatever they want. Hopefully that will be for their own RRSP or other investments to fund their retirement.

On a cash flow basis, even ignoring the fact that family #1's RRSP investments may do poorly, I'd much rather be family #2.

And there you have it. Cash flow is the key. Simply looking at a snapshot of wealth—net worth—can be misleading and lead to bad conclusions and faulty strategies. It can even lead to nightmare scenarios.

Of course, a simple strategy based on building a large net worth does work for some people: the enablers who happily accept our cash each and every day of our lives, guaranteeing themselves a sure-fire way to riches in the process.

MANY "WEALTHY" PEOPLE ARE LIVING A MIRAGE

The common accepted way to get "rich" is to focus on building assets. That means focusing on material things such as houses, stocks and other investments in RRSPs, TFSAs and regular investment accounts, as well as the value of businesses they may own.

It seems to me that many people who became millionaires (at least on paper) got rich by borrowing to do it. It sounds easy: take a loan from a bank, invest in something and hope the thing you buy grows in value faster than the interest you have to pay on the debt. In other words, their wealth is debt-dependent.

That may sound good, but basically many of them are living a mirage that could evaporate at any moment. What could happen? Well, pretty well any of the following:

- **The asset values may crash.** For example, the S&P TSX composite index, the key stock market measure in Canada, lost almost 50% of its value between June 2008 and March 2009.
- **Interest rates may rise.** In Canada today the prime rate (that is, the interest rate charged to the banks' best customers) is 3% per year. In the last 30 years it had only been lower from April 2009 to May 2010, when it was 2.25%. If the prime rate rises by a couple of percentage points, many millionaires will be hard-pressed to keep making the loan payments required to keep their lives afloat. For example, if the rate on an $800,000 25-year mortgage rose from 4% to 8%, the monthly payment would increase from $4,208 to $6,106. That's an increase of $1,898 a month which is a 45% rise. On an annual basis it would require $22,776 more a year to feed that pig. There is no doubt about it, the possibility of rising interest rates is a cash pig looming on the horizon.
- **They may have "liquidity" issues.** When it comes time to convert the assets to cash, will they be able to sell? In other words, will there be buyers willing to pay cash for the paper value of the assets? This could be a major problem in case of an economic downturn. If this happens it will be the luxury items that will be most difficult to sell. No one wants expensive toys when they are having problems buying the basic necessities of life. All those monster houses, sleek boats and vacation homes come to mind. These luxury items will become tough to unload as fewer and fewer people are able and willing to afford them. It's a simple case of too much supply and not enough demand

driving prices down. Some current millionaires could become non-millionaires overnight.

- **Cash Cow problems can happen to anyone.** Debt-fuelled millionaires have cash cows just like the rest of us. For some of them it's actually an inheritance from their parents. For others it is their business that they own and operate. But for many of them it's the same as it is for us regular people: themselves. If anything traumatic happens, such as losing their high-paying job or suffering some kind of injury that prevents them from earning the money needed to sustain their wealth, they have a serious problem.

So maybe some of the wealthy people you know are at risk. They may or may not know it, but my guess is that many of them are well aware that their house of cards may collapse one day.

WHY I DON'T WANT TO WIN THE LOTTERY

What about getting instantly wealthy? Maybe that's the answer, you may think.

I haven't won the lottery, but I have imagined what it would be like and have read about many people who have. Here's some food for thought.

We've all seen the ads. The freedom of never having to work again. The cash to buy whatever toys you want. Vacations multiple times a year.

Here's why I personally don't want to win the lottery:

- If you never needed to work again, it would take away the main incentive to get out of bed in the morning. You may find that having nothing to do becomes depressing after a while.
- After you win, you'd never know whether anyone you meet from that point on was being nice to you just because of your money.
- You would become a target for those people who want some of your money.

Now I know that this is not always the case. Many people who win the lottery get by just fine afterward. These people tend to be the ones who are quite well-adjusted in the first place. They have hobbies they enjoy. They tend to have solid family relationships. Some even keep their jobs, though they no longer need the money.

Hey, here's an interesting thought: maybe those people would have been happy even if they hadn't won the lottery.

GOING BEYOND THE NUMBERS

This book is about personal finance, but we all know that money isn't everything. I've made the case that spending our days trying to get rich is a risky strategy that often doesn't work. Even those that actually do reach millionaire status often find a new set of things to worry about—such as preserving their wealth.

It would seem to me that securing and increasing your cash flow is a far better strategy that would lead to a much better life.

So let's go beyond a simple finance book, shall we? Let's discuss the relationship between money and happiness. If wealth as measured by net worth does not necessarily make people happy, what does?

Does Money Buy Happiness?

That is a very interesting question, wouldn't you agree?

I'm tempted to say "no" but that would be too simplistic. In fact, I am pretty sure there is no single answer.

I think we could agree that for very poor people money could buy some happiness. Imagine you have kids to clothe and feed but you are so poor you can't afford to. That sadly is the miserable predicament of millions of people around the world. A few hundred dollars allowing them to survive would obviously make their dreams come true. They would probably become happy, or at least happier.

But what about a person who makes $100,000 per year, and lives in a nice house with a loving family? Would this person be happier if she or he made $125,000 per year? I don't know. I suspect it would depend on the person, and what he or she would have to do to earn the extra money.

To really address the question I figured I would ask someone who has money—lots of money. He is a multi-millionaire who was born and raised on a Saskatchewan farm. I'll call him Martin.

When I asked him to answer the question, "Does money buy happiness?" he rephrased it to "Can money bring happiness?" That is a much better question because it implies a more complex answer than "yes" or "no." Here is his story.

When he was young his family did not have much—no car, no telephone, no luxuries, a used bike. But they had plenty of food and adequate clothing. At that time in his life, his main source of entertainment was his dog Tip. He also loved playing sports, riding his bike and many other self-made activities. Martin was a happy child. Money, or the lack thereof, did not enter into his thinking.

When Martin was 15, tragedy struck. Both his parents perished in a blizzard.

He was sent to a Christian college in Regina where he was surrounded by other children, some of whom were from wealthy families. In this environment, he remembers being just as happy as any of his schoolmates.

After graduation from university and admission to two professions he became a businessman. The business prospered. There were many long days and weeks spent toiling over all the tasks that are required to build a successful business. The value of the business grew substantially and there was money available.

But his lifestyle changed very little during the time he was growing his business. He felt secure. Happiness did not come from the dream that someday he might become rich from the sale of the business, allowing him to quit work. It came from his work challenges in the manufacturing industry, family activities and outside activities, including sports.

Here are a few of Martin's observations on the subject of happiness:

- **Money is not necessarily required for happiness.** This is proven over and over again by very poor people who wake up happy every day.
- **Money is an enabler.** It allows us to do certain things that would otherwise be impossible.
- **Money can bring satisfaction.** It can give one a feeling of security and contentment. The opposite is also true: if one has debts and is unable to meet the commitment requirements, the lack of money can cause worry, anxiety and probably unhappiness.

Martin sold his business and became a multi-millionaire. He says happiness now comes in different ways. He finds much pleasure from sharing some of his wealth for the benefit of those less fortunate. He also devotes a large amount of time volunteering his time and expertise to causes that he believes in. He describes the happiness this brings him as a very special feeling.

Martin concludes with this: "Happiness must come from a group of values in a person's life such as career, family, friendship and realizing that if we are fortunate to have wealth it is incumbent on us to give to those who are less fortunate. So money, if properly used in a balanced way, can help bring us happiness."

There you have it—conclusions about the subject of happiness from someone who has been poor, and rich, but always happy.

What Causes Happiness?

I'm not what you'd call a naturally happy person. In fact, when I was young, I was often unhappy.

I remember a day in my twenties when I tried to figure out why I wasn't so happy. I sat down and drew a vertical line down the middle of a blank sheet of paper. The heading of the left column was "Good things about me" and the right was "Bad things about me." I then proceeded to list all the good things I could think of. There were 10. Then I started on the bad things side. Guess what? There were 12.

That process did not make me happy and I don't suggest you try this yourself!

What was making me unhappy? I didn't know. And I was clueless about what would make me happy. I read a lot of self-help books in those days trying to figure it out. I made some progress but it was not easy.

If you are like most people you never really bother to figure it out. Many people just muddle along with vague ideas about what might make them happy. Let's spend some time delving into the question, shall we?

"The Happy Movie"

My views on happiness changed the day I saw an awesome documentary film called *Happy* by Academy Award–nominated director Roko Belic. The film is a must-see if you are interested in discovering what might make you happy. You can find out more and view clips of it at www.thehappymovie.com.

The movie was inspired in 2005 when Hollywood director Tom Shadyac (*Bruce Almighty, Liar, Liar, Patch Adams*) read a *New York Times* article ranking the United States as 23rd in national happiness. He handed the article to Belic and asked him to find out why.

The movie answers the question by taking a fascinating journey in search of happy people from the bayous of Louisiana to the deserts of Namibia, from the beaches of Brazil to the villages of Okinawa. It asks, and answers, the following:

- Does money make you happy?
- Does work make you happy?
- If not, what does?

One section I found extremely interesting and useful featured prominent psychologists and neuroscientists. They have been studying people to find out what causes us to be happy.

They started with the obvious: do external things make us happy? They studied athletes who win the big prize. You would think that professional athletes who work hard and are fortunate enough to win the big prize would be happy as a result. Well, they are (surprise, surprise), but that happiness is often short-lived.

One of the key findings is that internal forces are much more important than external forces. They came to this conclusion by, among other things, studying identical twins. They found that happiness is caused by:

Source of Happiness

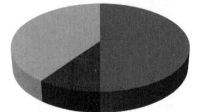

- Genetic (50%)
- External circumstances (10%)
- Intentional activity (40%)

Fifty percent is determined by who we are. We are born with a certain "genetic set point" and that is the state we tend to default to when there are no other factors influencing us. Some people are naturally happier than others.

The surprising finding was that only 10% of the happiness of people they studied came from external circumstances, in other words, what happens to them. This includes their type of job, income level, where they live, health, social status and age.

A full 40% is determined by what you choose to do. They found that physical activity is one key. Those who enjoy getting out and engaging in sports and other activities are generally happier than those who don't. This is for several reasons, including the fact that you can't focus on negative things while you are focused on trying to score a goal or not fall off your bike.

But it seems that your thoughts can also influence your level of happiness. That is, if you are willing to give it a try. The movie features a Buddhist monk who can literally increase his level of happiness at will as measured by a scan of his brain activity.

This is absolutely fascinating, useful information.

Happy for No Reason

That is the title of a book by Marci Shimoff (with Carol Kline). Shimoff is actually the narrator of the *Happy* movie, which is how I found her book.

She wrote the book after doing a survey of the people she knew. She found that the happiest people weren't the most successful and famous. Some were rich and some poor. Some were married and some single. Some even had health challenges. There seemed to be no logic to what made people happy. She then began to consider the question: "Could a person actually be happy for no reason?"

That set her on a quest to find experts on the subject. She also delved into research of the growing field of positive psychology, the scientific study of the positive traits that enable people to enjoy meaningful, fulfilling and happy lives.

She sought out and interviewed 100 happy people whom she calls the "Happy 100." She began asking everyone she met, "Who's the happiest person you know?"

The book summarizes her findings.

Her first major discovery centres on the idea that we all have a "happiness set-point" that the movie refers to as a genetic set-point. This she describes as the "genetic and learned tendency to remain at a certain level of happiness, similar to a thermostat setting on a furnace."[1]

Good news: she found that those of us who aren't lucky enough to have been born happy can actually change their happiness set-points. That also means that it may be possible to reduce the 50% genetic allocation for the source of happiness and increase the 40% that is due to intentional activity. In other words, it may be possible to have even more control over your happiness.

Shimoff tells the story of what she calls her big break. She says it began with a decision to take care of herself. Remember the last chapter where we discussed this? Here is a real-life example of another benefit to taking care of your biggest cash cow: you may become inspired.

She went on a seven-day silent retreat and came up with the idea for a new book: *Chicken Soup for the Woman's Soul.* Less than two years later, the book became a #1 *New York Times* best-seller and she then went on to write five more *Chicken Soup for the Soul* books that have sold more than 13 million copies.

That propelled her to national TV and radio shows, and speaking engagements where she addressed as many as 8,000 people at a time. She was treated royally wherever she went. People stood in line for hours for autographed copies of her books, many telling her that her books had changed or even saved their lives.

She was happy about the things in her life, but she wasn't really happy. She met many famous people along the way who weren't happy either.

Her quest for what makes people happy led her to one of her most amazing discoveries, "The Happiness Continuum." It summarizes the issue beautifully.

Think about this: we are always somewhere on a continuous scale of happiness from unhappy, to happy for a bad reason, to happy for a

---

[1] *Happy for No Reason*, Marci Shimoff with Carol Kline, Free Press, 2008.

good reason, to happy for no reason. Brilliant! Here's how she describes them:

- **Unhappy**. When you just feel down. Nothing seems fun and life is a hassle. Note that she makes it clear this doesn't include clinical depression, for which professional help is absolutely necessary.
- **Happy for a Bad Reason**. When people are unhappy, they tend to indulge in addictions and behaviours that may feel good for the moment but are ultimately detrimental. These include drugs, alcohol, compulsive gambling and excessive shopping, to name a few. This is not happiness, just a temporary masking of unhappiness.
- **Happy for a Good Reason**. This is what most people think of when they think of happiness. You have good relationships with family and friends, success in your career, financial security and a nice house and car. It's a feeling of happiness because you have healthy things that you want. But the problem is that it depends on external conditions. If the conditions change or are lost, you become unhappy. Conversely, it leads many people to remain unhappy until all the conditions are met. If they aren't, these people remain unhappy forever.
- **Happy for No Reason**. This is the key. It is true happiness, a neurological state of peace and well-being that isn't dependent on external circumstances.

When you are happy for no reason, you bring happiness to your outer experiences rather than trying to extract happiness from them. Your happiness is not contingent on everything in your life being just right.

As a logical person, I love this kind of book. It uses real life stories, expert evidence and simple logic to come to concrete conclusions that you can actually start using right away to improve your life. How can you beat that?

If you want to be happier, start your journey by renting the movie and buying the book.

My Take on Happy

Now, I am not a psychologist so please don't take the following as professional advice. These are just a few ideas that may help some people raise their happiness level a bit. Here goes.

I wish I could have seen the movie *Happy* and read *Happy for No Reason* when I was in my twenties. I'm sure they would have made a world of difference to me over the years.

Since seeing and reading them, I can honestly say that I feel happier more often. I am much less likely to let a bad mood dominate me for hours, which my genetic happiness set-point used to let happen too often. Simply knowing what is happening seems to have given me the power to make a change.

I also find that certain things can change my mood. Here are a few that seem to work for me.

Movies

I find that if I sit around not doing anything, I tend to think about problems that need resolving (but can't be easily resolved) and that makes me feel lousy. The obvious key is to do something to break the train of thought.

I love a good movie and find that if I set aside a couple of hours to go see one, either at home or at the theatre, it takes me away from that thinking. I am transported to wherever the movie takes place.

Music

I am not a musician, but I do love listening to music. As far as I'm concerned, the switch to digital music files was the best thing to happen in a long, long time. I was never a fan of buying and storing dozens of CDs (and, before that, records). Now I can have my whole music library on my iPhone to listen to it any time I want. If I hear a new song I can go to the iTunes store, buy it for 99 cents and be listening to it immediately.

I find I can't write while listening to music, but I find it perfect for exercising as it makes the time go by quickly.

What about you? What are your favourites? Are they close at hand for you to listen to when you want to break the cycle of your thinking?

Reading

Sitting down with a good book, whether paperback, hardcover or digital, is one of the best ways I know of to get my mind off things. Obviously the added benefit is that you can learn things!

Anticipation

This is an interesting concept. I find that scheduling future activities can be uplifting as you anticipate their arrival. If you plan ahead for something you like to do, for a concert in several weeks, let's say, focusing on the future pleasure may brighten your mood. In some cases the anticipation is better than the actual event, but even then you have experienced some pleasure—the pleasure of anticipation.

It seems to me that this is lost on many of the current generation. Life seems to be all about instant gratification. Kids want things and they want them now. Getting hooked on that may set them up to rarely experience the simple pleasure of anticipation.

What about you? Do you schedule pleasurable activities for the future so you can enjoy the anticipation of their arrival?

Being Around Up-beat People

Obviously this may not be easy to do, but don't you find that socializing with positive people helps your mood? I am always amazed by friends and acquaintances who seem to be "naturally happy" even when things aren't going so well for them. I wish I were like that, but the best alternative, I find, is being around people like that.

You have the power to increase your happiness if you want to. What have you got to lose by trying?

My Secret to Life

Just before I end this chapter, I'd like to share with you something that I believe can improve your life.

My family always groans when I remind them of it. "Here comes another 'Dave-ism'" is the common refrain. That's because they've heard me say it so many times, not because they disagree with it (at least I think that's the case!).

The secret became clear to me about a decade ago. I was stressed out almost every day at home and work as I tried to operate and grow my accounting practice, see to all of my kid-related duties, as well as write my first book, *Smoke and Mirrors: Financial Myths That Will Ruin Your Retirement Dreams.* There never seemed to be enough hours in the day. I was constantly worried about all the things that still needed to be done.

I had read that it is better to plan your activities on a weekly basis rather than a day at a time. Doing that helped, but I was still finding it difficult to get everything done. As a result, important things sometimes did not get done and I missed some deadlines.

Then one day I had a revelation. It seemed to me that the things that tended not to get done were usually the things I didn't like to do. Filling out accounting checklists, marketing activities and making certain phone calls were, and still are, not high on my list of things I like to do.

Things I did like to do, like writing, bookkeeping for my business (hey, I'm not weird, just an accountant, okay?) and organizing my office, always got done.

The problem was that doing all the things I liked to do often left no time for the things I didn't.

If that sounds like you, there is a simple answer. It is my secret to life:

Begin by doing what you don't want to do.

That's it. Begin each new set of activities, whether it is your personal life or your business life, with the thing that you know you should do but don't want to. If you do this, the important things will get done because you do them first and the less important things will get done simply because you like to do them.

Try it today. I have found it makes a world of difference both personally and professionally.

The key thing is to just start the activity. You will find that you won't feel like starting that task, but you'll usually discover that once you start it the task isn't as bad as you envisioned it would be.

Do this on a consistent basis and you'll be way more efficient and should feel better about yourself as you accomplish much more than you used to.

MILLION DOLLAR WRAP-UP

We all have different relationships and beliefs when it comes to money. There is therefore no "right answer" to where you need to be financially to make yourself happy. But what is clear is that slaving away and suffering to reach some magic dollar figure like a million dollar net worth will probably not bring happiness during the process and often doesn't for those who actually reach the target.

If, however, you live within your means, spending less than you bring in each month, you'll be well on your way to a fulfilling life of positive cash flow, with little or no debt—and those are good ingredients for happiness.

Life is not about the quest for "freedom" from the working world in our fifties. If you were actually able to do that, you would most likely find that you wouldn't like it after a while. It would probably become boring.

In my mind, life should be about enjoying the journey, not reaching the destination. If you equate "rich" with "happy" I encourage you to seek out and talk to someone you know who actually is rich. Ask for their advice. Most people are more than willing to spend time talking about themselves so I doubt this will be a problem.

Do they wake up thinking about how rich they are? Does this make them happy? What does?

You may find simply asking people what makes them happy often leads to interesting conversations and deeper friendships, both key happiness ingredients.

4

THE TRAP: WHY YOU AREN'T GETTING RICH AND THEY ARE

I understand that many people think they'd like to get rich. The problem is that most of them have no idea how to actually do it and that opens them up to become the source of other people's riches. In other words, they look for other people to make them rich—and actually end up poorer as a result.

I'll give you an example.

I am looking at a well-produced piece of junk mail that offers to teach me how to make money on the Internet. If I go to the free seminar, the self-made millionaire promises to reveal how I can generate income 24 hours a day, seven days a week, without a lot of technical experience, inventory, staff or headaches, from the comfort of my home.

My question is: if the person is so successful, why not just use the system to make millions from the comfort of his home? That's probably because it actually isn't that easy. It's easier for him to fill seminar rooms with people willing to give up their hard-earned cash to learn the "secret."

The people who offer the secrets to getting rich know that the key to riches is the cash flow. Seminars, at least successful seminars, bring in fees from the seminar itself but also from related things like book sales and newsletters of the seminar leader and his or her associates.

I am not saying that all seminars like these are designed to take advantage of you. Many might provide useful information. Just be wary.

From now on I'd like you to view anything that promises to make you rich quickly or easily with suspicion. It is highly likely that the people pitching you the idea actually do know how to get rich—by taking your money.

HOW THE BANKS MAKE MONEY

Think about it. Who knows how to make money better: you or your bank? Well, the bank has guaranteed cash flow from your pocket each and every day via bank charges, interest on your debts and through mutual fund fees, etc. What about you? How are you trying to get rich? By buying their investments or even borrowing from them to buy their investments? If so, you are falling into the trap.

The financial institutions make significant amounts of money because they know how to guarantee cash flow from their clients on a continuous basis. They aren't making the bulk of their money by investing in the stock market—they are receiving it in cash from you every minute of every day.

To a large degree banks make their money using OPM (that stands for Other People's Money). You know what? It's *your* money they're using.

Simply put, you deposit money in your bank account and they pay you a small amount of interest, say 1% per year. They then lend your money out to other customers at a higher rate—maybe a line of credit at prime plus 1%, which would currently be 4%. On your $10,000, they make a profit of 3% of $10,000, or $300 each year.

Why don't we turn the tables and learn how to get ahead financially from the institutions that know how to do it?

That means we focus on our cash flow today and for the rest of our lives.

PLUG THE CASH PIG LEAKS

In previous decades it was much easier to track your cash flow because life was simpler. You had a bank account in which you deposited money—your paycheque, for example—as well as any other sources of income. To spend that money you had to either withdraw cash or write a cheque. You simply could not spend more than you had in your account. If you tried, your cheque would bounce.

The major problem with spending today is that debt allows you to easily spend more than is in your account. Overdraft protection, often charging double-digit interest, is one culprit. Credit cards, however, are the major cause of this problem. It is just so easy to slap down the plastic to buy something. As a result, many people end up spending much more than they have earned. That is negative cash flow that you can't really see, since the excess of what you spend over what you can afford to pay off is just sitting on a credit card statement you don't really even have to look at.

The fact that many cards charge interest at 10% to 20% or even more just compounds the problem. They are adding $1,000 to $2,000 every year to a $10,000 credit card balance. That is cash outflow that you don't ever see unless you track your finances or at least look at your credit card statements.

Naturally we should also be focused on increasing our cash inflows, but generally it is much easier for people to control cash outflows than it is to find new sources of cash inflows. The key to the Cash Cow Strategy is to realize how much cash is going out, where it is going and then start to plug the leaks. To do otherwise is similar to trying to fill a bathtub with water without bothering to put the plug in. Much of your effort to bring more in is going down the drain.

Let's move on to some of the other big cash outflow leaks.

The Mutual Fund Fee Monster

I have said on many occasions that I am a fan of using a qualified, trustworthy investment advisor to handle your personal finances. I use one myself even though my family's investments are not that complicated. We don't even have any money in the stock market. But I still want an independent expert to watch out for us, make recommendations and handle all the administrative details, such as rolling over GICs and government bonds, etc. I am prepared to pay for this service and you should too.

What I am not a big fan of is expensive mutual funds that drain two or three percentage points of the net asset values each and every year to pay commissions to the various sellers in the system, among other things. This annual fee is called the Management Expense Ratio or MER.

This can be a huge drain on your investments. For example, say you started with $100,000 in your RRSP and invested it all in mutual fund A with an MER of 2.5% per year. If that mutual fund were able to achieve a 6% annual rate of return on its investments, without the MER it would grow to $320,713 in 20 years. If 2.5% a year were paid out in MER fees every year, the funds would only grow at 3.5% per year. The original $100,000 would only grow to $198,978. The difference, the total MER fees, would be $121,735.

The sellers and administrators of the mutual funds are using the Cash Cow Strategy. They earn their fees and pay for all the other suppliers to the fund, regardless of what happens to its value. Of course they make more if the fund does well, but they make good money each and every year regardless. They know how to make money.

For you, mutual fund fees are an absolute cash pig—continuous cash outflows that you don't even see. I have no problem with mutual funds that consistently beat their related index, but the problem is that many of them don't. It makes little sense to stay in an investment that charges high fees when there are alternatives like exchange-traded index funds with much lower expenses.

Borrowing to Get Rich: It Can Work, But Don't Bet on It

It sounds tempting, and I've even created a spreadsheet that makes a compelling case that borrowing to build wealth may work, especially if the debt is tax-deductible.

The problem is that for the average Canadian it is a dangerous strategy because the whole plan is based on debt. What if the asset (investments or perhaps real estate) declines in value and the bank won't renew the loan? You could lose it all. And you could lose it all quickly. I heard of a case in which someone was convinced to borrow $250,000 via an interest-only loan to invest in the stock market in June 2008—the peak of the market. Even if he was able to do as well as the S&P TSX composite index since then, his investments would now be worth around $200,000 since the index is still down about 20% in mid-2012. But the loan he took out still sits at $250,000.

The wealthy—usually those with high net worth, making good money—have a much greater chance of maintaining this strategy. That's because the banks love them. They make a lot of money off the interest the borrowers pay their whole lives. These people have power. Bank A won't renew the loan? No problem, they can just take all their business to Bank B, C or D. Any of them will be happy to take their money. We average folk aren't so fortunate. If we run into financial difficulty and can't keep servicing our debt, guess what? The game is often over.

The wealthy can (and an argument could be made that they must) continue the debt financing for a long time, in some cases forever. They are slaves to the financial institutions that hold their loans. That's fine; as long as they continue to bring in the cash to make the loan payments, they can maintain this illusion of wealth.

The reality is that in many cases their wealth is a house of cards. Are they really rich or is this an accident waiting to happen? Only the whims of the stock market, the housing market and their bankers know for sure.

The Wealth Effect Is the Enemy

The Wealth Effect is the idea that if people feel richer they will spend more money. This usually happens when house prices or the value of stocks and mutual funds are rising. People think about their increasing net worth and tend to go out and spend more money because they are worth more on paper.

The problem is that this is a terrible strategy. It is in fact the opposite of the Cash Cow Strategy. That is because it leads to cash spending based on unrealized paper gains.

The fact that your house value has increased should have no impact on how much you spend. That is because a higher house value does not give you a penny more in cash. You only realize the gain if you sell.

Similarly a rise in the stock market that manifests itself in a higher market value on your RRSP statement should not cause you to go out and spend more money. That is because it is an unrealized paper gain. To get at that money you'd have to cash in your investment, pay any deferred sales charges due on the mutual fund or commissions on any stock sales, withdraw the funds from your RRSP, and pay any tax that would be due. Then and only then would you have more cash to spend. But of course you'd be pillaging your retirement savings to do it.

The interesting thing is that in many cases of the Wealth Effect no one is forcing or encouraging people to spend more. They are doing it themselves because it seems to make sense. They think, "Hey, I am worth more so I deserve to go out and spend more on myself."

If there ever was a recipe for personal financial disaster, this would be one of the key ingredients. Just ask anyone who invested a lot of money in Internet stocks at the peak of the dot com boom. Many of these people saw future riches, increased their spending on disposable items, then found themselves with worthless stock and lots of debt soon after.

The potential disaster compounds itself if people are somehow convinced to borrow against the paper gains on their assets to allow them to spend more money now. They convince themselves that they could always pay back the borrowed money with the gains they've "made." But they haven't made the money yet—it is just temporary.

The problem is that the paper gains may not actually happen. They could disappear very quickly. But the debt doesn't. It has to be paid back somehow.

Think about those people in the U.S. who took out large home equity lines of credit in 2006 at the height of the U.S. housing boom. Today many of them are "under water" with houses worth less than the mortgage and other debt on them. That is the Wealth Effect at its most devastating.

The Wealth Effect should really be called the Wealth Defect. It is a huge cash pig since it encourages cash outflows without any real, tangible cash inflows to compensate.

SOMETIMES PEOPLE ARE THEIR OWN WORST ENEMIES

Sometimes the mistakes people make are not because they are being pushed by someone trying to make money off them. In these cases it is their own beliefs that cause them to adopt strategies or behave in a manner that drains their bank accounts. Here is one such story.

Paul's Story

I got an email from a gentleman I'll call Paul. Paul's predicament did not really stem from a desire to get rich quickly or easily by investing in real estate. There was no real estate broker pushing him to buy.

The first problem Paul had was rooted in his own belief that he could do as well as his parents had with their home, in their day.

But his problems really began from a sense of entitlement following years of self-sacrifice necessitated by the fact that he did not realize a large expected gain on his home like his parents did. In a nutshell, the cash flow required to finance his new life became very difficult to handle.

Here's the story in his own words...

I was born in 1958, which many would consider to be the tail end of the baby boom. In 1970, my parents purchased a 2,100 square foot house on a huge lot in Mississauga, Ontario, for $40,000 and sold it 16 years later for $265,000.

It was an astounding time of rapidly rising house prices, but it was also an era of high interest rates. Nevertheless, it seemed that purchasing a house was the route to take if I wanted to see an investment soar in value.

There was one substantial problem:

While I had graduated from university in 1983 with a manage-able student loan of $7,000 and immediately secured a public sector job, I did not have anything close to a decent down pay-ment saved six years later when I decided to buy my first house.

I had rented an apartment from 1983 to 1989 but despite sav-ing as much of my pay cheque as possible I still could not afford even a modest townhome in my new work location of Brampton, Ontario. House prices had continued to rise so rapidly that despite my modest salary increases every year I could not keep up with rocketing home prices.

Taking pity on me, and fearing I was destined to spend my life in rental oblivion, my mother offered to loan me $50,000, to be repaid with interest. I soon found a small townhouse listed for $200,000 and I approached a bank with my $50,000 down payment grasped firmly in hand, certain they would welcome me as a mortgage client. After all, I had a 25% down payment and a secure job.

I was about to be humbled.

The mortgage loans officer rejected my application, scoffed at my salary and suggested that if I ever wanted to purchase a house I had better start looking for potential tenants to help with the mortgage payments. The house I desired was located near a local community college.

The Catch-22 I faced, however, was trying to secure tenants without owning a rental house. The bank would not grant the mortgage loan without signed leases, but how was I to secure tenants without a house to rent?

In a bizarre series of events I went about advertising the house I did not yet own in the local community college's housing directory and showed the house to prospective student tenants from the outside only. After all, I didn't have the keys to a house I did not yet own!

Despite this, and thanks primarily to an extreme housing shortage for students, I soon had three signed leases and rental deposits. The loans officer then granted the mortgage and I quickly moved into the new house along with my three tenants.

I lived in the basement while the college students took one bedroom each on the top floor. Despite the less than ideal situation of sharing my new house with strangers, I felt I could now sit back and witness the same meteoric rise in house prices that my parents' generation (and, in fact, the early baby boomers) had enjoyed.

Right?

Wrong!

The ink had no sooner dried on my 1989 mortgage papers when house prices tanked. Prices quickly plummeted 25%. My $200,000 ticket to prosperity was now worth $150,000 and there it remained for several years.

When I sold it 16 years later, the house had not risen in value by over 560% as had my parents' house. It had risen in value a modest $25,000 and sold for $225,000. That was a gain of only 12.5% before factoring the costs to sell.

As the bestseller Boom, Bust and Echo *points out, demographics makes all the difference in one's life opportunities and experiences.*

I had learned a valuable lesson:

Just because something has happened in the past does not guarantee it will happen again in the future.

I sold my townhouse in 2005 but the mortgage was not paid off. I had built equity of about $150,000. With the interest on mortgages being front-end loaded I had discovered that despite regular monthly mortgage payments I had made only modest gains in repayment for the first few years.

I emerged from 16 years of being confined to the basement of my own townhouse, and I was determined to start living!

Just as the fast food jingle proclaims, "You deserve a break today," I felt I certainly deserved a break—but for much more than one day. After all, I had just lived through 16 years of tenants and endured dungeon-like surroundings, so watch out.

Nothing was going to stop me from making up for lost time, despite having only a $150,000 net worth. I contacted a mortgage broker and asked him to provide the topmost dollar amount for which I would qualify.

He did his calculations and informed me that I could buy a house valued up to $370,000.

I immediately searched for houses in a far more desirable (and expensive) neighbourhood than I was used to and soon purchased a house at the very ceiling of what I could afford. I was still single at the time but I was determined to tackle the mortgage without tenants sharing the premises.

I had a strong sense of entitlement and it knew no bounds! I went crazy!

The banks had now recognized my credit-worthiness and were falling over themselves offering me credit cards, lines of credit and mortgages. While I knew enough to avoid credit cards and their sky-high interest rates, I did apply for and received a huge $80,000 secured line of credit.

$80,000!! It felt as though I had just won a lottery.

Ignoring the fact that this amount would have to be repaid with interest I went on a spending spree. I soon squandered the equity built up over years in my first house. I was like a madman determined to reap the benefit of 16 years of self-sacrifice. I did not realize, or chose not to realize, that despite the 16 years of cellar-dwelling I had not reaped the same financial rewards of those home owners born 10 or more years before me.

Instead, I hired an interior decorator and bought only the best of high-end furniture. Painters were hired, decks built, carpets removed and hardwood flooring installed and professional landscaping performed. Money was spent so rapidly it was hard to keep track of where it was going. Of course, no driveway was complete without a beautiful vehicle so I purchased a brand new top-end SUV with steep monthly payments for the next four years.

My "Aha!" moment finally arrived in 2009. I had just exited an "original art" gallery, having placed a deposit and arranged monthly payments for a $10,000 framed work of art. It was a "must have" for my dining room!

Or was it?

I walked to my rapidly depreciating SUV, stepped inside, closed the door and immediately felt nauseated.

This latest expenditure had not brought pleasure. Instead I felt pain.

I was forced to ask myself, "What are you doing?"

The realization of how I had overcompensated for my years of denial finally sank in.

It was about this time that a close friend loaned me his copy of a book that he highly recommended. The title was Smoke and Mirrors, *and it was written by David Trahair. The book emphasized the importance of paying down a mortgage.*

I started reading other personal finance books. I watched television programs such as Gail Vaz-Oxlade's Til Debt Do Us Part, *with its common-sense approach to debt repayment, complete with money budgeting jars.*

What a wake-up call!

I had enjoyed a ride on a well-greased debt slide but now found myself at the bottom facing the daunting task of clamouring back up.

I had now learned yet another lesson, perhaps the ultimate lesson:

One does not rise up a slippery slide at anything near the speed of descent.

Years of commitment and laser-like focus on debt repayment lay before me.

I immediately traded in my SUV for a small, used economy car. The home renovations and improvements stopped. A boarder was found to rent the basement and I found an additional source of income with a part-time job. I consolidated my line of credit with my mortgage loan to create one monster loan upon which I could devote 100% focus and repayment effort. The interest rates on mortgage loans were at historic lows but I was no longer naive enough to tempt fortune. I realized that with a mortgage renewal could come higher interest rates. I secured a 5-year mortgage at 3.79% and began to tackle Goliath.

I then took a Bristol board, drew a series of connecting squares in a "Snakes and Ladders" fashion (minus the snakes and ladders). Each square was to be coloured in once a $1,000 mortgage principal payment was made. At the end of the lengthy path was a huge bubble representing complete mortgage pay-off.

The poster represented a visual goal of the end objective— paying off the mortgage as rapidly as possible. The Bristol board poster was now placed on a bedroom wall as a daily visual reminder for my wife and I of how, if we can make it through several years of self-sacrifice, the end objective will be reached.

Each year since the creation of the poster I have phoned my mortgage provider on the mortgage anniversary date and requested that he increase deductions from my bank account to maximize the principal repayment. The mortgage payments are made weekly.

There is not much money left over after paying other household expenses such as house and car insurance, utilities, car repairs, gasoline, cable, etc., but we are determined to pay the mortgage off as rapidly as possible.

My wife and I are on our way. With our joint commitment and focus we are making steady progress in paying off the mortgage and years of debt accumulation.

I'll leave the last word to Paul: "It's all about self-discipline. While I knew better, I nevertheless indulged recklessly and am now paying the piper."

I am grateful that Paul shared his story with me so that I can share it with you. If some of Paul's story sounds a bit like your life, the ball is now in your court. You can learn the best way there is—from someone else's mistakes—and change your ways now, or you can follow down the slippery slide to ruined dreams and crushing debt.

CLOSING THE TRAP

Let's stop trying to get ahead by playing the game—and losing. Let's forget the idea that we are going to get ahead easily or quickly, and get back to reality. That simply means focusing on bringing more cash into our lives and watching where it goes so we can keep more of it and live the life we desire.

5

THE DREAM OF HOME OWNERSHIP

We've always been told that real estate is a sure-fire way to build wealth. After all, they aren't making any more of it, right? This simple kind of logic has resulted in more than a few people getting into real estate for the wrong reasons.

Let me give you an example.

I went to a seminar about how to get rich, put on by a well-known organization. The ads played upon the fact that the stock market in Canada has been performing poorly over the last few years and if you attended this seminar, you'd find out how to build wealth without having to worry about the machinations of the stock exchange. That sounded interesting, so I went.

The seminar leader began with this:

"Ladies and gentleman, I want you to get out a piece of paper and a pen and write down 'I will purchase a property within six months of this seminar.' Or, if you already own a property, 'I will purchase a second property within six months.'"

This was in early 2012 and I thought to myself, "Is this guy serious? I think he's from the United States, but does he not know that more than 25% of U.S. single family occupied dwellings are 'under water' or worth less than the mortgage owing on them?" Buying real estate without the proper due diligence and financial analysis has been devastating for millions of Americans. It's even caught many who did all the right things but just got stuck with simple bad timing.

Well, he was serious.

Don't have a good credit rating? No problem, just Google "hard money loans" and you can find thousands of people to lend you money. It may cost you 12% a year but, hey, you want to get into the housing market, right?

How did he get started in real estate since he didn't have any money for a down payment? He got creative—he remembered he had a free credit card offer with a $20,000 limit. He used this credit card for the down payment. "He can't still be serious, can he?" I quizzed myself.

When another attendee dared to bring up the legitimate issue of capital gains tax on the sale of real estate (for rental properties, not principal residences), the guy gave a short answer and stated that the next person who interrupted his presentation would be asked to leave.

If you want to really get rich, commit to purchasing a rental property every six months for the next five years, we were told.

This is the type of sales pitch that leads many people down a path of financial ruin. It truly is a case of "buyer beware" when it comes to using real estate to get "rich."

I should say that for some people buying a rental property may actually be a good strategy. If a suitable property is purchased at the right time and responsible tenants are consistently found, the rental income helps pay off the mortgage and eventually it can become a cash cow. But becoming a landlord is not for everyone. For those with little prior experience and inadequate resources to maintain the property, the recommendation to buy anyway makes little sense.

THE WEALTHY BARBER WEIGHS IN

Like many people, I devoured every page of *The Wealthy Barber*, the epic personal finance book written by David Chilton, when it first came out in 1989.

For those of you who don't already know, David has now published a new book called *The Wealthy Barber Returns, Significantly Older and Marginally Wiser*. If you read the first book, you have to read this one. If you didn't read the first book, you have to read this one.

Here's what he says about home ownership in a chapter titled "Under House Arrest":[1]

...after 30 years of studying thousands of people's finances, I've come to realize the following piece of advice is absolutely key to achieving your financial goals: Live in a house you can truly afford.

He then goes on to support the case later in the chapter:

Two of the finest minds in personal finance, Charles Farrell (Your Money Ratios) and Thomas J. Stanley (The Millionaire Next Door) argue that overspending on one's home may be the single biggest inhibitor to achieving financial independence.

Interestingly, he goes on to address the issue of happiness when it comes to home ownership:

The funny thing is that people who live in homes they can truly afford consistently rank very highly in happiness surveys. Perhaps they didn't stretch because they were already content or maybe they were content because they didn't stretch. That cause-and-effect stuff is always tricky. But I suspect it's a combination of both.

He sums up the issue as only he can:

Look, I love home ownership, but make sure it's you that owns the home and not the other way around.

I agree 100%. Home ownership is what everyone dreams of—a piece of real estate you can call your own. But it has to be within your budget.

How Much Home Can You Afford?

Many people convince themselves that by buying a home they are "building home equity." The bigger the home, the more equity they

---

[1] *The Wealthy Barber Returns, Significantly Older and Marginally Wiser: Dave Chilton Offers His Unique Perspectives on the World of Money*, David Chilton, Financial Awareness Corp: 2011.

build, right? Not necessarily. The problem is they often have not thought about the cash flow implications of paying for and maintaining the large home. Remember a house is usually a cash pig. Many of these people have not crunched the numbers and figured out if they will ever pay off the mortgage. Even more importantly, they have not thought about the annual cost of those higher property taxes, maintenance costs, insurance and utilities—not to mention the monthly carrying cost of the mortgage itself.

The first thing to realize is that just because you qualify for a mortgage does not mean you can afford it. That is because the financial institutions generally use ratios that compare housing costs to household income. The problem is that these ratios ignore the age of the purchaser and therefore can be misleading. Let's explore the issue.

Gross Debt Service Ratio

The GDS ratio says that your monthly housing costs should not exceed 32% of your gross household monthly income which is your combined salaries before any deductions like income taxes, CPP and EI. If either you or your spouse is self-employed, it is gross sales less any business expenses before other deductions. You also include any other sources of income like investments and non-employment income. Your housing costs include mortgage payments (principal plus interest), property taxes and heating expenses.

Total Debt Service Ratio

The TDS ratio states that your monthly debt load should not be more than 40% of your gross monthly income. Your monthly debt load includes mortgage payments and other debt payments like car loans, credit cards, lines of credit and student loans.

The Age Factor

Assuming you are on side with respect to these ratios, and obviously you should be, you then need to think about your age. How many years are there between the time you take on the mortgage and retirement?

Say you are 40 years old and plan on retiring at age 65. That is 25 years, the maximum amortization period you can now spread a mortgage over according to new CMHC rules that came into effect July 9, 2012. If you meet both ratios above, you are probably in pretty good shape. But what about a 50-year-old planning to retire at 65? There is only 15 years to go before retirement. If that person takes on a mortgage with a 25-year amortization period, the mortgage would not be paid off until age 75—10 years after retirement.

I have been studying the issue of retirement for a long time and the conclusion I have come to is that you simply must retire without a mortgage. In fact retiring totally debt-free is the best and the safest way to retire well. To do otherwise is to bring a large cash pig into retirement with you. It's going to be a real strain to feed that pig, or those pigs if you also have other debt, on a fixed income.

So when you try to figure out how much house you can afford, use a maximum amortization period equal to the number of years between purchase date and the planned date of your retirement. Only then will using the above ratios be meaningful.

CMHC Homebuying Calculators

The maximum price you can afford depends on several factors other than household income like the amount you have for a down payment, the interest rate on the mortgage and you other debt payments and housing costs.

Canada Mortgage and Housing Corporation provides a significant amount of excellent information to help potential home buyers with their decision at http://www.cmhc-schl.gc.ca/en/co/buho/buho_005.cfm. One of the tools available is the Mortgage Affordability Calculator. Let's use it for the following example:

- Gross monthly household income $16,666 ($200,000 annually)
- Monthly debt payments $2,000
- Monthly property taxes $416 ($5,000 annually)
- Monthly condominium fees $500
- Monthly heating costs $140
- Down payment $200,000
- Mortgage interest rate   4.0%
- Amortization period   25 years

So what do you think a couple that are aged 40, with a $200,000 down payment and want to retire at age 65 can afford? The answer is:

- A maximum mortgage of $733,888

With a $200,000 down payment that means a house worth $933,888.

The maximum mortgage represents the maximum mortgage permitted with the down payment provided, or the maximum permitted given your income and debt obligations.

In this case the maximum mortgage is 3.66 times the annual household income and that seems reasonable.

The people who are getting into trouble are assuming mortgages that are much higher than that—some are even able to find lenders willing to loan 10 or more times annual household income. Don't put yourself in this position. Use the CMHC calculator to see what your limit should be.

If you are planning to buy a home, or upgrade your existing one, for goodness' sake make sure you can afford it. If you don't, your dream could very well become your nightmare.

RENT IS NOT A FOUR-LETTER WORD

Let's face it, we rarely hear anyone bragging about the fact that they are renting their home. Renting is looked down upon. "The rich don't rent," we often hear. Well, what if that isn't necessarily the case? What if it is possible that renting the place where you live is a better financial option than buying?

Let's explore how this may be true.

First of all, when analyzing renting versus buying, many people just focus on the monthly mortgage payments versus the monthly rental payments. With the ultra-low interest rates available today, mortgage payments often look low, even in the range of what it would cost to rent a similar dwelling, so the question posed is why throw your money away in rent when you can "build equity" by buying?

But this simple comparison is missing vital pieces of the information and that can lead to huge problems. For example, since renting should cost you less than buying, there will be less cash outflow. That will put you in the enviable position of deciding what to do with the extra cash that is not going into the house. You could top up your RRSP or TFSA, and actually build some savings.

The best way I know of to answer the rent-or-buy question is to create a spreadsheet so that you can play with different inputs and assumptions that often have a significant effect on the answer.

I have created one that you can download and use for free. Just go to www.trahair.com and click on the "Cash Cows, Pigs and Jackpots" link on the left side of the home page. The spreadsheet is the "House Rent versus Buy Analyzer" and it is a totally unprotected Microsoft Excel file.

You'll note there are different "Tabs" at the bottom of the screen that you can click on to go to separate sections of the same spreadsheet as follows:

- **Home.** This tells you a bit about the spreadsheet, including the version number and what it does.
- **Questions.** This is where you answer all the questions needed to do the comparison. Note that this is the key tab: you can come back and change any of your answers to see what the effect on the decision is.
- **Results-Summary TFSA.** This shows you all the cash costs of the rent and the buy options, year-by-year for up to 25 years. It factors in the effect of inflation and concludes by calculating the difference between the ending after-tax values of your TFSA and regular investment value with the rent option versus the tax-free proceeds on the sale of your house after real-estate commissions. It only includes results for years 1, 10, 20 and 25.
- **Results-Detail TFSA.** This shows you all that the Results-Summary TFSA tab shows, but also includes details for each of the 25 years.
- **Results-Summary RRSP.** This shows you all the cash costs of the rent and the buy options, year-by-year for up to 25 years. It factors in the effect of inflation and calculates the ending value of your RRSP investments each year up to year 25 and the amount of cash in hand you would receive after cashing in and paying tax on your RRSP at that time. It also shows the ending after-tax value of your regular investment account. It then compares the

total cash in hand after cashing in your RRSP and the value of your tax-paid regular investment accounts to the tax-free proceeds on the sale of your house after real-estate commissions. It only includes results for years 1, 10, 20 and 25.

- **Results-Detail RRSP.** This shows you all that the Results-Summary RRSP tab shows, but also includes details for each of the 25 years.
- **Assumptions.** These are the assumptions that went into the spreadsheet.
- **Loan.** This tab will show you the annual calculations regarding the mortgage loan used to purchase the house.

The following is a screen shot of the home screen of the House Rent versus Buy Analyzer:

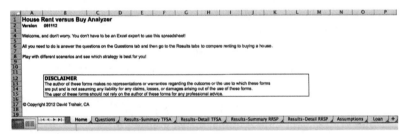

© Copyright 2012 David Trahair, CA

Note the tabs at the bottom. The Home tab is the active tab and is shown in bold at the bottom.

To illustrate how the calculator works, I've created an example.

WARNING: Please note that this example is NOT my answer to the question as to whether renting is better than buying! It is simply for illustrative purposes so that we can have a meaningful discussion about the numbers and other vital issues that should go into the decision.

The intention is not for you to zero in on the numbers in the example. What I am hoping you will do, whether you are a real estate agent, a loan officer or someone trying to decide whether to buy a house or condo, is download the free spreadsheet, use your own figures and come to your own conclusions.

Please don't obsess over whether the sample estimate for annual heating costs is the right figure!

An Example—123 Any Street, Hometown

Here are all the details I entered on the Questions tab on the spreadsheet:

GENERAL

What is today's date?	05/13/2012
What is the property address?	123 Any Street, Hometown

RENT OPTION QUESTIONS

What amount will you need to put as a last month's rent deposit?	$3,500
What is the monthly rental payment?	$3,500
What amount per month will you have to pay for utilities (heat and hydro) if any?	$300
At what annual rate do you think your utilities will increase by?	2.00%
What is the term of the lease (in years)?	25
At what annual rate do you think your rental payments will increase by?	1.00%
What is the combined amount of your and your spouse's unused RRSP deduction room at the start? (Look at each of your Notices of Assessment for the last year's personal tax return.)	$80,000
What are your and your spouse's combined future year's annual RRSP deduction limits estimated to be? (It is generally 18% of your prior year's earned income to a maximum of $22,450 each in 2011 and $22,970 each in 2012.)	$36,000
What is the average marginal income tax rate for you and your spouse? (This is the rate of tax you would pay on each additional dollar of income and the refund rate for RRSP contributions.)	40.00%
What is the average marginal income tax rate of you and your spouse estimated to be when you cash in your RRSP?	40.00%
How much can you and your spouse contribute to a Tax-Free Savings Account (TFSA) at the start?	$40,000

(NOTE: Each Canadian adult 18 and over can contribute $5,000 per year since 2009.)

How much can you and your spouse contribute to a TFSA each year?	$10,000

(NOTE: Enter $5,000 if you don't have a spouse or $10,000 if you do.)

At what annual rate do you think your TFSA will increase by?	3.00%
At what annual rate do you think your RRSP will increase by?	3.00%
At what annual rate do you think your investments outside your TFSA will increase by after taxes?	2.50%

BUY OPTION QUESTIONS

What is the purchase price of the house (including HST for new houses)?	$800,000
What will other closing costs be (land transfer tax, legal fees, mortgage loan insurance, etc.)?	$30,000
What amount do you have for a down payment and closing costs on the purchase?	$200,000
What is the annual interest rate on the mortgage?	4.00%
What is the amortization period of the mortgage (maximum 25 years).	25
At what annual rate do you think your house value will increase by?	2.00%
What real estate commission rate do you think you will pay on the sale of your house?	5.0%
What are the annual property taxes estimated to be in the first year?	$7,000
What are the property insurance premiums estimated to be in the first year?	$2,000
What are the annual maintenance costs estimated to be?	$5,000
What are the estimated annual heating (oil or gas) costs?	$2,400
What are the estimated annual hydro (electricity) costs?	$1,200
At what annual rate do you think your property taxes, maintenance, heat and hydro payments will increase by?	2.00%

Here is a screen shot of the Questions tab of the spreadsheet:

	A	B	C	D	E	F	G	H	I	J	K	L	M
1	**House Rent versus Buy Analyzer Questions**												
2												Your	
3	Answer these questions in column L:											Answers	
4													
5	GENERAL												
6	What is today's date?											5-13-12	
7	(e.g., 5-13-2012)												
8													
9	What is the property address?											123 Any Street, Hometown	
10	(e.g., 123 Any Street, Hometown)												
11													
12													
13	RENT OPTION QUESTIONS												
14	What amount will you need to put as a last month's rent deposit?											$3,500	
15													
16	What is the monthly rental payment?											$3,500	
17													
18	What amount per month will you have to pay for utilities (heat and hydro) if any?											$300	
19													
20	At what annual rate do you think your utilities will increase by?											2.00%	
21													
22	What is the term of the lease (in years)?											25	
23													
24	At what annual rate do you think your rental payments will increase by?											1.00%	
25													
26	What is the combined amount of you and your spouse's unused RRSP deduction room at the start?											$80,000	
27	(Look at each of your Notice of Assessment for the last year's personal tax return)												
28													
29	What are you and your spouse's combined future years' annual RRSP deduction limits estimated to be?											$36,000	
30	(It is generally 18% of your prior year's earned income to a max of $22,450 each in 2011 and $22,970 each in 2012)												
31													
32	What is the average marginal income tax rate for you and your spouse?											40.00%	
33	(This is the rate of tax you would pay on each additional dollar of income and the refund rate for RRSP contributions)												
34													
35	What is the average marginal income tax rate of you and your spouse estimated to be when you cash in your RRSP?											40.00%	
36													
37	How much can you and your spouse contribute to a Tax Free Savings Account (TFSA) at the start?											$40,000	
38	(NOTE: Each Canadian adult 18 and over can contribute $5,000 per year since 2009)												
39													
40	How much can you and your spouse contribute to a TFSA each year?											$10,000	
41	(NOTE: Enter $5,000 if you don't have a spouse/common law partner or $10,000 if you do)												
42													
43	At what annual rate do you think your TFSA will increase by?											3.00%	
44													
45	At what annual rate do you think your RRSP will increase by?											3.00%	
46													
47	At what annual rate do you think your investments outside your TFSA will increase by after taxes?											2.50%	
48													
49													
50	BUY OPTION QUESTIONS												
51	What is the purchase price of the house (including HST for new houses)?											$800,000	
52													
53	What will other closing costs be? (land transfer tax, legal fees, mortgage loan insurance, etc.)											$30,000	
54													
55	What amount do you have for a down payment and closing costs on the purchase?											$200,000	
56													
57	What is the annual interest rate on the mortgage?											4.00%	
58													
59	What is the amortization period of the mortgage (maximum 25 years)?											25	
60													
61	At what annual rate do you think your house value will increase by?											2.00%	
62													
63	What real estate commission rate do you think you will pay on the sale of your house?											5.00%	
64													
65	What are the annual property taxes estimated to be in the first year?											$7,000	
66													
67	What are the property insurance premiums estimated to be in the first year?											$2,000	
68													
69	What are the annual maintenance costs estimated to be?											$5,000	
70													
71	What are the estimated annual heating (oil or gas) costs?											$2,400	
72													
73	What are the estimated annual hydro (electricity) costs?											$1,200	
74													
75	At what annual rate do you think your property taxes, maintenance, heat and hydro payments will increase by?											2.00%	
76													
77													

Home | **Questions** | Results-Summary TFSA | Results-Detail TFSA | Results-Summary RRSP | Results-Detail RRSP | Assump

123 Any Street: The Assumptions

To get an idea of what it costs to rent a house, I did a Google search for house rentals in the Toronto area and found kijiji (www.kijiji.ca) to be very helpful. I found the following unfurnished detached home in north Toronto available for $3,500 per month plus utilities:

- completely renovated, backing onto a ravine;
- walking distance to good schools, a shopping plaza, a community centre;
- 3 + 1 bedrooms, 2 bathrooms;
- finished basement with gas fireplace and separate entrance;
- use of stainless steel fridge, stove, dishwasher, microwave and washer and dryer;
- forced air gas with central vacuum;
- carport with parking for three cars.

Since the house was not for sale, the cost to buy it was not available so I had to make an educated guess. As anyone who is familiar with housing prices knows, the market in much of Toronto in early 2012 is, well, crazy. This is the place where in January 2012 more than two dozen potential buyers lined up for the chance to buy a well-worn, detached, three-storey brick house listed for $995,000. The six-bedroom house on a 33- by 118-foot lot ended up selling for $1,111,000.

So what would our sample house sell for? Hard to tell, but let's be conservative and say $800,000. I have also assumed that closing costs including land transfer tax and legal fees totalled $30,000, so the total costs to buy the house came to $830,000.

Annual costs during the first year are estimated as above and are all projected to rise at a rate of 2% per year.

I have assumed there is $200,000 available for a down payment and closing costs. So the amount of the mortgage would be $630,000 since $30,000 of the cash was required for the closing costs leaving $170,000 for the down payment.

Don't Forget the Closing Costs

Many people don't plan for all the closing and other costs they may have to pay on buying a home. These costs usually can't be added to the mortgage—you'll have to have the funds available to create a bank draft or certified cheque. These can include:

- legal fees;
- land transfer tax;
- prepaid property taxes and utility bills (to pay the vendor for amounts paid covering the period after the sale);
- moving costs (if you are moving from another location);
- HST, GST and PST as applicable.

It is generally recommended that buyers budget between 1.5% and 4.0% of the purchase price for closing costs. On the $800,000 home we are using in our example that would be between $12,000 and $32,000. As you can see I have input $30,000, which is 3.75% of the purchase price.

Land Transfer Tax

Land transfer tax can amount to a large sum that you need to be prepared for. All provinces have a land transfer tax except Alberta and Saskatchewan, which levy a smaller transfer fee. In most cases the tax is based on a percentage of the selling price. Homebuyers in Toronto also incur an additional municipal land transfer tax.

Here are the current (May 2012) Ontario land transfer rates based on the purchase price of the home:

First $55,000	0.5%
$55,001 to $250,000	1.0%
$250,001 to $400,000	1.5%
Over $400,000	2.0%

So the Ontario land transfer tax on our $800,000 house would be $12,475 if it was not in Toronto. Since it is in Toronto, which uses a similar graduated scale of rates based on the purchase price, add $11,725 in municipal land transfer tax for a total of $24,200. For further information, www.ratehub.ca has an excellent land transfer tax calculator for all provinces and territories that also factors in any first-time buyer rebates.

GST/HST

If you buy a new or substantially renovated house, including a residential condominium unit, a duplex or a mobile home from a builder, you will have to pay GST or HST on the purchase price.

Here is a summary of the GST/HST rates for the province after July 1, 2010:

B.C.	HST at 12%*
New Brunswick	HST at 13%
Newfoundland and Labrador	HST at 13%
Nova Scotia	HST at 15%
Ontario	HST at 13%
Other provinces and territories	GST at 5%

* Note that B.C is returning to the GST and PST effective April 1, 2013.

There is a federal GST/HST housing rebate available under certain conditions. This rebate allows individuals (not corporations or partnerships) to recover some of the GST or federal part of the HST paid for a new or substantially renovated house that is for use as the individual's (or their relation's) primary place of residence.

Your primary place of residence is generally a house that you own and that you intend to live in on a permanent basis. You may have more than one residence, but you are considered to only have one primary place of residence.

Under current rules, new home buyers can apply for a 36% rebate of the GST or federal portion of HST applicable to the purchase price to a maximum of $6,300 for homes costing $350,000 or less. For new homes priced between $350,000 and $450,000, the rebate would be reduced proportionately. New homes priced above $450,000 would not receive a federal rebate.

Details are available in Form RC4028–GST/HST New Housing Rebate available on the CRA website (www.cra-arc.gc.ca) that includes information on the provinces that offer provincial rebates and copies of the forms you need to file.

For example, buyers of new homes in Ontario may receive rebates of 75% of the provincial portion of the HST applicable on the purchase up to a maximum of $24,000 if they paid HST on the purchase of the land and $16,080 if they did not.

In B.C. the maximum rebate amount depends on the date that construction or substantial renovation of the home becomes substantially complete, the date you file your rebate application and whether you paid HST on the purchase of the land. Under proposed changes the maximum B.C. new housing rebate would increase to $42,500 if you paid HST on the purchase of the land, and $28,475 if you did not.

Note that if you buy, build or substantially renovate housing to rent for long-term residential use by individuals as their primary place of residence, you are not entitled to claim the new housing rebate but you may be eligible to claim the GST/HST new residential property rebate.

The GST/HST rebate rates, conditions and other related issues are complex and constantly changing. Make sure you research the current rules and consult with knowledgeable real estate professionals before making any purchase decisions or claims.

Other Costs after Closing

Remember there may also be other costs shortly after you move in such as furniture and appliances (especially if you are moving to a larger house), utility hook-up fees and painting and cleaning.

A Word About the Down Payment

If you can afford to put down at least 20% of the value of the house you are buying, you'll have a conventional mortgage.

With a down payment of less than 20% of the purchase price of your home, you'll have what's called a high-ratio mortgage. In this case in Canada today you are then required to have the mortgage insured. That means you have to pay an insurance premium to protect the lender in case you default on your mortgage. It's called mortgage loan insurance or mortgage default insurance.

There are currently three organizations that provide mortgage insurance: Canada Mortgage and Housing Corporation (CMHC), Genworth Financial and Canada Guaranty Mortgage Insurance Company. Your lender will generally make arrangements for the mortgage insurance, pay the premiums and pass them on to you. In most cases the one-time premium can be added to your mortgage and therefore paid over time.

With mortgage insurance the terminology revolves around the "Loan-to-Value." That is, the financing required versus the value of the house or its cost. So a 20% down payment is a Loan-to-Value ratio of 80%.

Here is a table of CMHC premiums for various Loan-to-Value ratios ranging from 80% to 95%. Note that if you are self-employed and can't provide third-party validation of your income, the premiums are higher and only available to a Loan-to-Value ratio up to and including 90%.

CHMC Mortgage Loan Insurance Premiums

Loan-to-Value Ratio	Down Payment Percentage	Standard Premium	Self-employed without 3rd-Party Income Validation Premium
75.1 to 80%	20 to 24.9%	1.00%	1.64%
80.1 to 85%	15 to 19.9%	1.75%	2.90%
85.1 to 90%	10 to 14.9%	2.00%	4.75%
90.1 to 95%	5 to 9.9%	2.75%	N/A

The above chart is for amortization periods up to 25 years. It is interesting to note that CMHC offers mortgage insurance on Loan-to-Value ratios of less than 80%. As you can see from the table above, the 1% standard premium applies for ratios from 75.1% up to 80%. That would mean a down payment of between 20% and 24.9%.

According to CMHC, the standard premium for Loan-to-Value ratios between 65.1% and 75% is 0.65% and 1% for self-employed without third-party income validation. For Loan-to-Value ratios up to and including 65% the rates are 0.5% and 0.8% respectively. This is what's called

"Portfolio Insurance" which "provides lenders with the ability to purchase insurance on pools of previously uninsured low-ratio mortgages"[2] according to the CMHC. It is not a requirement for borrowers, so you only have to worry about paying premiums if you are over 80% Loan-to-Value ratio.

In our example, $200,000 is available. Closing costs will take $30,000 of that, leaving $170,000 for the down payment. Therefore the mortgage required is $630,000. The Loan-to-Value ratio is 78.75% ($630,000/$800,000) and therefore mortgage loan insurance is not required.

Remember that HST or PST (as applicable) is due on the premiums and must be paid on closing as the tax can't be added to the mortgage.

CMHC Changes

On June 21, 2012 the federal government tightened the rules on high-ratio mortgages to try and cool the housing market and prevent people from becoming over-extended. The government has announced four measures for government-backed insured mortgages with loan-to-value ratios of more than 80% that came into effect on July 9, 2012:

- Reduction in the amortization period to 25 years from 30 years. The maximum was 35 years in 2008 and was reduced to 30 years in 2011.
- The maximum amount Canadians can borrow when refinancing reduced to 80% from 85% of the value of their homes.
- The maximum gross debt service ratio fixed at 39% and the maximum total debt service ratio fixed at 44%.
- The availability of government-backed insured mortgages limited to homes with a purchase price of less than $1 million.

Many people have been throwing caution to the wind and extending themselves with way too much mortgage debt. All these rules are being implemented to try and reduce the amount of debt people can take to realize the dream of owning their own homes. The dream is fine but it has to be affordable.

---

[2] http://www.cmhc-schl.gc.ca/en/corp/nero/nero_019.cfm

THE KEY POINTS THAT MOST PEOPLE MISS

Remember when I said that many people doing a comparison of renting versus buying just compare the monthly mortgage payments to what the monthly rental payments would be? In this case the monthly rental payments are $3,500. The Loan tab on the spreadsheet calculates the monthly mortgage loan payments. In this case they turn out to be $3,325.

Buying wins, right? Wrong! That is focusing on one single number and that often leads to totally misleading conclusions.

Sure, the monthly mortgage payment amount is significant but what about all the other numbers? Try changing the down payment on the spreadsheet. I just reduced the cash available for the down payment and closing costs to $100,000 from $200,000 and the monthly mortgage amount rose to $3,853.

So let's move into the other numbers and issues that need to be considered.

The Opportunity Cost

In our sample scenario, the buyer had to come up with $200,000 from somewhere to be able to purchase the house. Where did that money come from? Was the buyer actually able to save that amount of money over the years? Or maybe a generous parent helped out with an interest-free loan or gift?

However that money was raised, the key point is that if this person was a renter instead of a buyer, that money would be available for other things—such as investing. This is the key point that many people ignore. It's the "opportunity cost" of the money. In other words, if the person did not sink the $200,000 into a house, what would happen to the money?

Tax-Free Savings Accounts (TFSAs)

In order to do an apples-versus-apples comparison on the spreadsheet, I've focused on one of the best tax breaks available to Canadians—the Tax-Free Savings Account or TFSA.

Beginning in 2009 any Canadian resident individual (other than a trust) 18 years of age or older can contribute up to $5,000 each year to a TFSA. The contributions are not tax-deductible, but the income earned in the TFSA is never taxed. This is a key advantage to anyone with excess funds available, such as the person we are talking about.

You'll see that in your case, the spreadsheet needs to know if it's you on your own or if you would be living with someone who can also contribute to a TFSA. That person could be a spouse, a common-law partner, or just a boyfriend or girlfriend.

Throughout the spreadsheet I have simply referred to this other person as your spouse to keep the wording to a minimum.

This is an important point. For example in the case of a TFSA it needs to know how much of the excess money can be sheltered each year from tax in a TFSA if you choose to rent. Whether the answer is $5,000 (if you live alone) or $10,000 (if you live with someone) will have a significant effect on the results.

Any excess funds (over and above what you are allowed to put in your TFSA) I have assumed would go into a regular investment account and would be taxed each year at rates depending on the specific investment mix. Note that the spreadsheet asks for the average rate of return you expect to make on the investment account after taxes. This is so the end result—the total investment value at the end of the 25-year period—can be combined with the value of your TFSA and be compared to the amount you would have received on the sale of your house (after real estate commissions). As most people are aware, the capital gain on the sale of your principal residence is not taxed.

Registered Retirement Savings Plans (RRSPs)

The other excellent tax break we have in Canada are Registered Retirement Savings Plans (RRSPs). The complicating factor with RRSPs is how to handle the tax effect. As you know, we get to deduct our RRSP contributions within certain limits. The limit for 2012, for example, is $22,970 and for 2013 it's $23,820. But the resulting tax refund we receive as a result of the contribution is a temporary one. We have to pay back the tax when we cash in our RRSPs. That presents us with some issues. What marginal tax rate do we use to calculate the tax refund? What do we do with it in terms of reinvestment? To be fair we must assume the refund is reinvested in the RRSP and not spent, right? And how do we deal with the end amount that is taxed upon withdrawal?

You'll see that the spreadsheet needs to know what you think the answers are to all these questions.

Since we are dealing with TFSAs and RRSPs, there is an interesting side benefit to this spreadsheet, which is really designed to help us make the decision between renting or buying a home. That benefit is that it can also be used to determine whether investing in a TFSA or an RRSP is the better option.

The Ongoing Cash Costs

The cash outflows required to maintain a house is another key point that needs to be addressed. For example, if you rent you may or may not have to pay utilities including heat and electricity. If you own you will definitely have to, but you'll also have to pay other ongoing costs that renters usually don't. These costs include property taxes, insurance on the building and repair and maintenance. As you can see, the spreadsheet needs you to estimate these amounts for the first year as well as the amount by which they will increase yearly.

CONSUMER DEBT WARNING

The previous section and the spreadsheet both assume there is cash available for the down payment and closing costs and to cover the annual costs of carrying the house under the buy option.

If you, or anyone you know who is considering buying a house, has a consumer debt balance before the purchase of a house, stop and think about what you are getting into. Your life after the purchase could become your worst nightmare.

That is because you are already in debt and therefore the additional costs of buying and paying for your home is going to cost you more—possibly a lot more. You are effectively adding the interest rate you are paying on your existing consumer debt every year to every dollar.

Consumer debt includes credit cards, lines of credit, car loans, etc. Say you have a $5,000 credit card balance you can't seem to pay off at an annual interest rate of 10% a year and a $5,000 line of credit at 5% a year. The extra $750 a year (an average rate of 7.5% a year on $10,000) is not factored into the spreadsheet.

If you've got consumer debt at a higher rate, which is possible with some credit cards, the situation is even worse.

If you've got consumer debt, the answer is simple: don't even consider buying a house until you clear the debt to zero.

COMPOUNDING CONFUSION

When it comes to compound interest with respect to investments, it's relatively straight forward. Compounding simply refers to how often interest is added to the investment and therefore interest going forward is calculated on the amount of the investment, plus the interest. For example, if we start with an investment of $100,000 on January 1 and earn interest at a rate of 6% per year compounded annually, our investment would grow by $6,000 to a value if $106,000 at December 31. That is $100,000 × 1.06.

If the interest was instead compounded semi-annually (twice per year), the $100,000 would grow by 3% to the middle of the year (by one half of the 6% annual rate). The $103,000 would then grow by 3% for the last half of the year to $106,090. That is $103,000 × 1.03. So with semi-annual compounding we end with $90 extra after one year due to the effect of earning interest on the interest.

But with mortgages, we are not starting with an investment, we are starting with a loan, so the situation is the reverse of our investments. Our financial institution, however, does have an investment in the loan to us, but since we are making monthly payments according to an amortization schedule that will pay the mortgage off over a number of years (under current rules you can go up to 25), it gets confusing.

Note that by Canadian law, fixed-rate mortgages (those with a fixed interest rate for the term of the loan, which is usually three or five years) must be compounded semi-annually. The fact that most mortgage payments are made monthly but are compounded semi-annually makes the calculations very complicated.

To illustrate this issue, I punched in a simple example into a mortgage program freely available on-line (just Google "mortgage amortization calculator Canada" but make sure it is one that will show the full amortization schedule of principal and interest for each payment). The mortgage amount was $100,000, the annual interest rate was 6% and the amortization period was 25 years (300 monthly payments). The monthly mortgage payment came to $639.81. The first payment at the end of the first month after the mortgage was advanced showed $493.86 of interest and $145.95 of principal for the total payment of $639.81. If this was a regular non-mortgage loan with interest compounding monthly, the first month's interest would be $500. That would be 6% divided by 12 equals 0.5% per month and $100,000 times 0.5% equals $500.

So why is the amount, according the calculator, only $493.86, which is less than $500, meaning a lower rate is being used? It's because the lender is not allowed to compound the rate monthly; they can only compound semi-annually. This forces them to use a lower rate. They calculate it like this:

A 6% annual rate compounded semi-annually is an "effective interest rate (EIR)" of 6.09%. Remember our investment example? $100,000 at 6% compounded semi-annually grew to $106,090 and that is 6.09% not 6%. So the lender uses an effective interest rate, instead of the stated rate. But since the payments are made monthly they need to use an interest rate that when compounded monthly would yield an effective interest rate of 6.09%. That happens to be a monthly rate of 0.49386%. In other words if you started with $100,000 and multiplied it by 1.0049386 and took the result and multiplied that by the same rate 11 more times you would end up with $106,090. Go ahead and try it on a calculator.

It is important to note that mortgages with variable rates, often referred to as adjustable-rate mortgages (ARMs) and lines of credit are not limited by the semi-annual compounding and usually compound on a monthly basis consistent with the payment frequency. To keep the example and the spreadsheet simple, I have assumed that the mortgage is a variable-rate mortgage with monthly compounding.

123 ANY STREET: THE TFSA RESULTS

So let's take a look at the next chart. It shows the results for 123 Any Street over the next 25 years. We'll start by looking at the first-year results for the rent option. You can see the last month's rent deposit of $3,500, then the annual rent payments of $42,000 (12 × $3,500). Since utilities are not included and we have estimated them at $300 a month we can see the annual cost of $3,600. The total cash outflow for the rent option is therefore $49,100.

The buy option has more items, including the down payment of $200,000, closing costs of $30,000, mortgage loan principal and interest costs of $14,977 and $24,927 respectively, property taxes of $7,000, insurance on the house $2,000, repairs and maintenance of $5,000, heating costs of $2,400 and electricity costs of $1,200. The total cash outflows in the first year are $287,504. That is $238,404 more than the rent option.

The couple in our example has never contributed to a TFSA before and therefore has $40,000 of room available in 2012 since each of them can save $5,000 per year starting in 2009 and they have not done so. Therefore $40,000 of the excess money they did not use to buy a house goes into their TFSAs. That leaves $198,404 to go into their regular investment account. You can see that after one year the TFSA has grown by 3% to $41,200 and the regular investment account value has grown by 2.5% to $203,364. Remember we are assuming that is

House Rent vs Buy TFSA Summary

Year	2012	2021	2031	2036
Year #	1	10	20	25
RENT				
Rent Costs:				
Down payment	3,500			(3,500)
Rental payments	42,000	45,934	50,739	53,327
Heat, hydro	3,600	4,301	5,244	5,790
Total Rent Costs (A)	**49,100**	**50,235**	**55,983**	**55,617**
RENT Values				
TFSA				
Opening	0	143,783	310,583	411,335
Contribution	40,000	10,000	9,565	10,000
Growth (tax free)	1,200	4,613	9,604	12,640
Closing	**41,200**	**158,396**	**329,752**	**433,975**
INVESTMENT ACCOUNT				
Opening	0	259,498	335,132	379,171
Contribution	198,404	703	0	2,600
Growth (after tax)	4,960	6,505	8,378	9,544
Closing	**203,364**	**266,706**	**343,510**	**391,315**
TOTAL TFSA and Investment Account (C)	**244,564**	**425,102**	**673,262**	**825,290**
BUY				
Buy Costs:				
Down payment	200,000			
Closing costs	30,000			
Principal payments	14,977	21,454	31,985	39,053
Interest payments	24,927	18,450	7,920	851
Property taxes	7,000	8,368	10,200	11,261

Year	2012	2021	2031	2036
Year #	1	10	20	25
Insurance	2,000	2,390	2,915	3,218
Repairs and maintenance	5,000	5,975	7,284	8,044
Heating (Oil and gas)	2,400	2,868	3,497	3,861
Electricity (Hydro)	1,200	1,433	1,747	1,929
Total Buy Costs (B)	**287,504**	**60,938**	**65,548**	**68,217**
ANNUAL EXCESS COSTS OF BUY (A−B)	**(238,404)**	**(10,703)**	**(9,565)**	**(12,600)**

BUY Values
HOUSE VALUE

Opening	800,000	956,074	1,165,450	1,286,751
Growth	16,000	19,121	23,309	25,735
Closing	**816,000**	**975,195**	**1,188,759**	**1,312,486**
Mortgage balance	**615,023**	**449,564**	**180,565**	**0**
EQUITY IN HOUSE (D)	**200,977**	**525,631**	**1,008,194**	**1,312,486**
EXCESS (DEFICIENT) VALUE EQUITY IN HOUSE (D−C)	**(43,587)**	**100,529**	**334,932**	**487,196**

Proceeds on sale of home	**1,312,486**
Real estate commission on sale	**65,624**
Net proceeds from sale of house	**1,246,862**
EXCESS (DEFICIENT) CASH ON SALE OF HOUSE	**421,572**

the rate after any investment fees and income taxes so this money is available to use at any time.

The total value of the couple's TFSA and investment account at the end of year one was $244,564.

What about the buy option? There are no excess funds since they have all gone to purchase the house and pay for the annual costs. The house has risen in value by $16,000, which is the 2% entered on the Questions tab. The mortgage balance at the end of year one is $615,023. That is the original amount of $630,000 less the principal payments during the year of $14,977. So the equity in the house is $200,977. This is the market value of $816,000 less the mortgage principal balance owing of $615,023.

So after year one the renters would be ahead by $43,587. In other words, the equity in the house is less than the total value of the renters' TFSA and investments by that amount.

The actual spreadsheet has columns for each year on the Results-Detail TFSA tab. The Results-Summary TFSA tab just shows years 1, 10, 20 and 25 as shown in the chart.

After year 10, the buy option has overtaken the rent option and shows the equity in the house to exceed the renters' investments by $100,529. After 20 years the homebuyers appear to be ahead by $334,932 and after 25 years the equity in their house is estimated to exceed the renters' investments by $487,196.

If they sold their house after year 25 for the estimated value of $1,312,486 and paid real estate commissions of $65,624 (at a rate of 5.0% as per the answer on the Questions tab) they would be left with cash of $1,246,862 which is $421,572 more than the $825,290 that the renters would have built up in their tax-paid investments.

123 ANY STREET: THE RRSP RESULTS

What if we used our RRSPs instead of our TFSAs to invest the extra funds?

In this example I have assumed that the renters' combined current RRSP deduction room is $80,000 and that each year another $36,000 of RRSP deduction room becomes available. I have also assumed they have marginal income tax rates that average 40% currently and that in 25 years when they withdraw their RRSPs their marginal tax rates will be the same 40%. Furthermore I have assumed the RRSP investments will grow at the same rate the TFSAs are expected to grow at, which is 3% annually.

Let's take a look at the next chart. It shows the summary RRSP results for 123 Any Street.

The buy option results are the same as the TFSA scenario as you would expect since we have not changed any of the inputs relating to the purchase of the home. It still shows the net proceeds from the sale of the house after 25 years to be $1,246,862.

The big difference is the RRSP versus the TFSA value after 25 years. As you can see, the combined RRSP values are estimated to be $876,078 but that is before taxes have been paid on any withdrawal. At a marginal tax rate of 40%, $350,431 in taxes would be owed (ouch!) leaving $525,647. Combine that with the $293,674 in the tax-paid investment account and you have a total of $819,321 in available cash.

That is $427,541 less than the buy option with $1,246,862. This is very close to the result we got with the TFSA strategy where the buy option won by $421,572.

PLAYING WITH THE INPUTS

Now let's use the power of the spreadsheet to see what the effect of different assumptions has on the results. You'll see that even small changes can have a significant effect on the outcome.

Housing Prices Increases

We have assumed a 2% annual increase in the value of the house over the next 25 years. That has increased its value from $800,000 to $1,312,485. What if the markets aren't so kind and the increase is only 1% per year?

The buy option still wins, but only by $149,359 for the TFSA option and $155,328 for the RRSP option instead of $421,572 and $427,541 respectively.

House Price

What if the couple got into a bidding war and ended up paying $1 million for the house instead of $800,000? With the same closing costs and down payment, and assuming it still grew in value by 2% per year, the buy

House Rent vs Buy RRSP Summary

	Year	2012	2021	2031	2036
	Year #	1	10	20	25
RENT					
Rent Costs:					
Down payment		3,500			(3,500)
Rental payments		42,000	45,934	50,739	53,327
Heat, hydro		3,600	4,301	5,244	5,790
Total Rent Costs (A)		**49,100**	**50,235**	**55,983**	**55,617**
RENT Values					
RRSP					
Opening		0	328,124	643,269	831,796
Contribution - current year		80,000	10,703	9,565	12,600
Contribution - prior year refund		0	7,293	6,492	6,165
Growth (tax free)		2,400	10,384	19,780	25,517
Closing		**82,400**	**356,504**	**679,106**	**876,078**
Tax on cashing in RRSP					**350,431**
Cash on hand after RRSP cash-in (X)					**525,647**
INVESTMENT ACCOUNT					
Opening		0	197,826	253,234	286,511
Contribution		158,404	0	0	0
Growth (after tax)		3,960	4,946	6,331	7,163
Closing (Y)		**162,364**	**202,772**	**259,565**	**293,674**
TOTAL RRSP and Investment Account		**244,764**	**559,276**	**938,671**	**1,169,752**
TOTAL Cash and Investment Account (X+Y)					**819,321**

Year	2012	2021	2031	2036
Year #	1	10	20	25
BUY				
Buy Costs:				
Down payment	200,000			
Closing costs	30,000			
Principal payments	14,977	21,454	31,985	39,053
Interest payments	24,927	18,450	7,920	851
Property taxes	7,000	8,368	10,200	11,261
Insurance	2,000	2,390	2,915	3,218
Repairs and maintenance	5,000	5,975	7,284	8,044
Heating (Oil and gas)	2,400	2,868	3,497	3,861
Electricity (Hydro)	1,200	1,433	1,747	1,929
Total Buy Costs (B)	**287,504**	**60,938**	**65,548**	**68,217**
ANNUAL EXCESS COSTS OF BUY (A−B)	**(238,404)**	**(10,703)**	**(9,565)**	**(12,600)**
BUY Values				
HOUSE VALUE				
Opening	800,000	956,074	1,165,450	1,286,751
Growth	16,000	19,121	23,309	25,735
Closing	**816,000**	**975,195**	**1,188,759**	**1,312,486**
Mortgage balance	**615,023**	**449,564**	**180,565**	**0**
EQUITY IN HOUSE (D)	**200,977**	**525,631**	**1,008,194**	**1,312,486**
EXCESS (DEFICIENT) VALUE EQUITY IN HOUSE (D−C)	**(43,787)**	**(33,645)**	**69,523**	**142,734**
Proceeds on sale of home				**1,312,486**
Real estate commission on sale				**65,624**
Net proceeds from sale of house				**1,246,862**
EXCESS (DEFICIENT) CASH ON SALE OF HOUSE				**427,541**

option still wins but only by $289,653 for the TFSA option and $283,405 for the RRSP option.

If the house only grew by 1% per year, the buy option loses to the TFSA option by $50,615 and the RRSP option by $56,863.

Interest Rates

What if interest rates don't remain at the current lows and the mortgage loan rates average 6% a year instead of 4% over the next 25 years? If we go back to a 2% annual increase in the value of the $800,000 house, the buy option wins by $113,209 over the TFSA and $110,704 over the RRSP.

If we assume only a 1% per annum average house price increase and 6% average interest rates on the mortgage, the TFSA option wins by $159,004 and the RRSP option wins by $161,509.

But there is another impact to rising interest rates. With the rent option, if we assume the excess funds available to the renters are invested conservatively—say, in Guaranteed Investment Certificates (GICs)—rising interest rates would mean better returns on the renters' investments.

If mortgage loan rates rise by 2% to 6% it would seem reasonable that GIC returns might increase by a similar amount. If we increase the assumed rate of return on the TFSAs and the RRSPs (which both grow tax-free, remember) from 3% to 5% and the rate of return on the regular investment account after investment fees and income taxes from 2.5% to 3.5%, guess what?

Assuming the house rises in value by 2% a year, the renters end up ahead after 25 years by $203,222 for the TFSA option and $280,403 for the RRSP option.

If we keep the annual increase in the house price to 1% per year, the TFSA renters end up ahead by the very significant amount—$475,435—and the RRSP renters win by even more—$552,616.

BEWARE THOSE TRYING TO SELL YOU SOMETHING

Be careful of those people trying to sell you something. For example, say I was trying to convince you that renting is the better option because I make my living selling investments. I might enter a lofty figure for the assumed rate of return on your investments and a higher mortgage interest rate. For example, say we assume you'll make 7% and 5.5% per year on your TFSA/RRSP and investment account respectively and that long-term 25-year mortgage rates will average 6%. With our original $800,000 house appreciating at 2% per year, the rent option beats the buy option by a whopping $859,646 for the TFSA and $961,018 for the RRSP.

The overall message here is that the picture is only 100% clear after the fact—when all the variables can be calculated as realities rather than guesses. Don't be fooled into relying on overly optimistic projections.

BEYOND THE NUMBERS

It has become clear to me over the years that when addressing any issue regarding personal finances that there is never one "right answer." That is why I create spreadsheets such as the one we have been using. With tools like this it is possible to go through an infinite number of scenarios—all you have to do is play with the answers to the questions. That is obviously an essential exercise.

The problem is that no matter how much thought you give to the inputs, no matter how many variations you try, no matter how many historical statistics you analyze, there is no guarantee that the future will look anything like your spreadsheet.

Life has a habit of throwing curveballs at us. Sometimes these are things that have never even happened before. Let's explore this in more detail.

Long-Term House Prices

Unfortunately, house prices generally do not rise on a consistent annual basis. In fact, it is possible that houses could actually lose value, even over a significant period of time.

All you have to do is look to the United States over the past few years to see proof of this. According to Zillow.com, a website that tracks U.S. housing data, as of December 2011 national home values had fallen 24% since their peak in 2006. On a national average basis, home values are back to late 2003 levels. That is more than eight years of zero growth with no significant recovery predicted any time soon.

And that is the major risk of the buy option: there is no guarantee that your house will appreciate at the rate you hope it will.

You could, however, make the case that the renters' investment rate of return is not set in stone either and that is a fair point. But consider the following scenario: What if you had a crystal ball back in 2003 and you knew that over the next eight years your house would be worth only what it was then? According to the spreadsheet, if I put in 0% rate of annual increase in our $800,000 home and left the TFSA and investment returns at 3% and 2.5% respectively, the TFSA renters' investments would be worth $381,934.

The home would still be worth $800,000 and the mortgage balance owing would be $491,633 leaving equity in the home of $308,367. The renters would be ahead by $73,567, even ignoring real estate fees to sell the house.

But consider the situation of the renter if there is a downturn in the market and house prices fall like they have in the U.S. With a good chunk of available cash in their TFSAs and investment accounts they would be in an excellent position to buy a home at a bargain price.

Repairs and Maintenance

The spreadsheet asks you to estimate the annual costs of repairs and maintenance in the first year and to enter the amount you think those costs will increase by on an annual basis. This is to cover all the regular costs like the protection/maintenance plan on the furnace and air conditioner, possibly the landscaping and snow removal contracts and window washing, etc. (unless you do all those yourself), as well as the major costs.

The major costs are the real issue. Over a 25-year period you are going to have some major expenses. The roof shingles will need to be replaced. You will probably need a new furnace at some point. The same goes for the air conditioner if you have one.

Some homeowners are unfortunate enough to have other unforeseen expenses that are significant. This is especially prevalent with older homes. Maybe the electrical wiring needs replacing. Or maybe there is a conversion from oil to gas heating. Or maybe the basement leaks, requiring extensive waterproofing to be done. These costs are often significant and require large lump sums of cash. The point is to make sure you are aware that these costs are coming and to build them into the spreadsheet, and your budget.

Renovations

If you are like many homeowners, you'll probably find it tough to resist the lure of making improvements to your home. Maybe it's finishing the basement this year, or renovating the kitchen, or maybe adding a pool. While this will improve your surroundings, it will usually cost a significant amount of money. Even if this increases the value of your home, it will definitely increase the current cash costs of living in your home—that is, it will have an impact on your cash flow.

If you plan a renovation, make sure you build the added cost into the spreadsheet. Without proper planning, an extensive renovation can turn a cash pig into a cash hog.

The End Game: Can You Sell?

Going back to our original example, we saw that after 25 years, the TFSA renters had $825,290 in their after-tax investments and the RRSP renters had $819,321 after cashing in their RRSPs and paying the tax.

The house owners had a house worth $1,312,486 that would yield $1,246,862 after real estate commissions to sell it.

But how easy will it be to sell your house for what you project it will be worth? That is worth giving considerable thought to. We know that demographics in Canada are changing. The baby boomers are approaching retirement and that means there will be more people retired than entering the workforce, having children and buying larger houses. Who is going to buy all the houses coming onto the market when you wish to sell yours?

The ability to sell, or cash in, is called "liquidity." This may become the most important factor of all in the years to come. Keep it in mind as you make decisions about your housing going forward.

CONCLUSION

It's most people's dream to own their own home. But the reality is that for some people it doesn't make sense. They simply don't have the cash flow to afford the purchase and the maintenance. If you are a renter in this situation, don't rush into buying a home. Your dream could become a cash pig nightmare from which it may be very difficult to escape.

Take the advice of David Chilton, author of *The Wealthy Barber Returns*, and only buy a home if you can afford to without stretching yourself financially. Download the House Rent versus Buy spreadsheet free from my website at www.trahair.com to see what the opening and ongoing costs are likely to be. Use the CMHC mortgage affordability calculator to see what maximum mortgage you should accept. And don't commit to the cash pig of a home you can't afford.

THE CONDOMINIUM CONUNDRUM

I don't know what it's like where you live, but today in early 2012 in the Toronto area, it seems the condominium or condo craze is at its peak.

While driving around downtown, or to the north, east or west of the city, you'll see cranes raising new condos all over the place and dozens of sites surrounded by hoardings, where planned condo construction has not yet begun.

Now let me be clear. I am not a real estate agent and I don't sell condos. I am also not opposed to the idea of buying a condo. It seems to me that buying a condo might be a viable option for renters who dream of owning their own home. It sure seems to be a better option than taking on a monster mortgage to buy a traditional home that is way out of affordable range.

But condos are not like houses where you own a piece of land. As a result the old maxim that "they aren't making any more real estate" does not apply to condos. They are making more of them, in some areas many more. And that makes the decision to buy more difficult because you could have a lot more competition when it comes time to sell yours.

The advantage of a house on a plot of land is that the land itself has value—in some cases, quite a bit of value. There are currently small bungalows on good-size lots in north Toronto that are worth in excess of half a million dollars. The buyers are not interested in the house—they want the lots. The first thing they usually do, in fact, is tear down the existing house and then build a custom home on the lot.

So with a traditional high-rise condo you don't have that inherent value to fall back on. That doesn't make them a bad idea; it just means you need to be extra careful before committing to buying one.

If you are a renter considering the major decision whether to purchase your own condo, this chapter is designed for you. After reading it you should have a much better idea whether it makes sense for you.

The same applies to you if you are considering investing in a condo as a rental property. Don't jump in before going through the numbers and considering all the other factors. Just like a house, a condo will usually be a cash pig for years after you buy it—just make sure it's a cash pig you can afford.

Let's dig deeper.

CONDO BASICS

I can understand the lure of a condo. They are generally less expensive than a traditional home. They often are low-maintenance—no more mowing the lawn or shovelling the driveway! Many have party and exercise rooms, and 24-hour security is often provided. But there are many things that need to be considered—before you buy.

CMHC has produced an excellent resource for potential condo buyers. It is called the *Condominium Buyers' Guide*. It's available on-line at no charge, and I highly recommend that anyone considering the purchase of a condo read it, cover to cover.

Definition of a Condominium

According to the guide a condominium is a form of legal ownership that is often used for high-rise residential buildings but can also apply to townhouse complexes, low-rise buildings and even individual houses.

Condominiums consist of two basic parts. The first part is made up of the individual private dwellings called "units" which are each owned and registered in the name of the purchaser of the unit. The second part is the "common elements" of the building. This includes all the areas other than the units, including things such as:

- the front lobby;
- hallways and elevators;
- recreational facilities (gyms, pools, etc.);
- walkways and gardens;
- mechanical and electrical elements.

The ownership of the common elements is shared by the unit owners and therefore they are responsible for the costs of maintaining and operating them.

The ownership interest in the common elements is an important factor to consider because the costs of maintaining them are charged to the unit holders in the form of monthly fees. The "unit factor" is usually calculated as the value of the unit compared to the value of all the units in the condo. Therefore, the owners of larger units pay more than the owners of the smaller ones.

The Legal Details

The creation and regulation of condominiums is regulated by provincial and territorial legislation and municipal guidelines. The condominium corporation itself will also have bylaws and rules that govern its operation.

The management of the condo's business affairs is generally the responsibility of a board of directors that is elected by, and usually made up of, unit owners. Each unit owner has the right to vote at meetings and the voting rights often are in proportion to the unit factor.

Condominium Regulations

Each province and territory has its own rules and regulations that govern the registry, construction and operation of condos. It is obviously a good idea to become familiar with these rules before buying a condo in your area. You could start by doing an Internet search for "condominium act, province" where you enter your own province or territory.

Each condominium will also have its own set of rules, regulations and bylaws to ensure that the property is operated effectively and fairly. Some may be very strict and some quite flexible. These rules cover things such as restrictions on the number of people per unit, whether pets are allowed, noise restrictions, what you can put on your balcony, and so on.

The rules of each condo should be clearly laid out in its governing documents and should be available from the vendor (seller), the board of directors or the property manager. Obviously, if you are planning to invest and live in a condo, you had better find out what the rules are, prior to buying, to make sure they suit your living style.

The Fees

Most condominiums require that unit owners pay monthly condominium fees to cover such things as the operation, cleaning and maintenance of the common areas, common area utility bills, operation and repair of the hot water heating and air conditioning systems, snow and garbage removal and salaries of the security staff, as well as other costs.

These monthly fees also usually include an amount to contribute to a "reserve fund" to cover the cost of major repairs and maintenance, such as resurfacing the parking lot, for example.

If the reserve fund is insufficient there may also be mandatory charges for unforeseen repairs to the condo's common areas.

A property manager is usually hired to oversee the administration of maintaining the common areas. It is important to note that this is not always the case. Some condos prefer to handle the maintenance themselves. These are referred to as "self-managed" condominiums. In this case the board of directors, and in some cases volunteers who are residents or owners, assume responsibility for the administration of the condo. Make sure you are aware of which operating style the condo is using and that you are comfortable with that style before you buy.

Who Pays for What?

The condominium's governing documents should spell out what ongoing charges are the responsibility of the unit owners and what falls to the condominium corporation. The CMHC guide lists the following as usually the responsibility of the unit owner:

- internal unit plumbing, appliances, heating, air-conditioning or electrical systems that are contained in and serve that unit;
- cleaning window surfaces that are accessible from inside the unit;
- cleaning some parts of the common elements, such as balconies and patios that are assigned to, or for the exclusive use of, the unit holder.

The condominium corporation is usually on the hook for:

- common plumbing, electrical, heating and air-conditioning systems;
- roof and wall repairs;
- window and door repairs and replacement;
- grass cutting and watering;
- recreational facilities;
- parking areas;
- any other part of the property that is not part of the unit.

Note that in some cases the costs are shared. For example, the heating and air-conditioning system may be part of the common elements, but the unit holder might be responsible for some tasks, such as changing the filters.

Insurance

The unit holders and the condominium corporation must have insurance as dictated by the specific laws of the province or territory. The condominium corporation bears the most responsibility in this area, which usually includes insuring:

- common area and units;
- the corporation's property such as furniture, equipment and any vehicles they may own;

- personal liability against claims for bodily injury and property damage occurring on the condominium's property or caused by some act or omission of the condominium corporation;
- boilers and other equipment, such as elevators;
- directors' and officers' insurance to cover them in case of a claim against them personally;
- all perils as dictated by the condo's governing documents.

Individual unit holders are usually responsible for insuring:

- personal property contents such as appliances, furniture, electronics and jewellery, as well as items stored in lockers;
- improvements made to the unit such as installing new cabinets;
- personal liability.

Renting Out the Unit

Many people purchase a condominium as an investment to rent out to other people. Most condominiums allow this, but did you know that some might not? If this is your plan, make sure you first conduct a thorough review of the official condominium governing documents and provincial or territorial legislation.

Condo Costs

Let's face it: a condominium is usually a cash pig, just like a traditional house on a plot of land. And just like a traditional house, it has the potential for a jackpot at the end if it has risen in value and you can sell it.

If you plan to rent it out, it may actually become a cash cow after you've paid for it. The problem is that this may be a long way off. You need to consider whether it makes sense to carry the costs of the investment (including the lost opportunity costs) until such time as the unit is paid off.

We need to dig into the numbers to decide whether to take the leap and become a condo owner and also to compare the alternatives once we have decided to buy one.

The Purchase Price

The cost of a new condominium often includes many other items besides the cost of the unit—items that you don't have to worry about if you buy a used condominium. For example, you may be responsible for:

- GST or HST on the purchase price;
- upgrades to the base unit (this is often negotiable);
- a parking spot (if you need one);
- development charges;
- PST or HST on appliances and other items being purchased with the unit;
- utility hook-up fees;
- landscaping fees;
- sometimes two months' common expenses toward the reserve fund (depending on the province or territory);
- occupancy fees (from occupancy closing to title closing), which may include estimated common expenses based on the disclosure statement budget, estimated property taxes and any interest due on closing;
- legal fees and disbursements;
- land transfer tax; and
- warranty program enrolment fees.

All the costs in addition to the unit purchase price should be clearly outlined in the agreement of purchase and sale.

The Monthly Costs

After you cover the purchase price, you'll need to budget for the following ongoing costs:

- mortgage payments;
- property taxes;
- condominium fees (also known as common expenses);
- unit and contents insurance;
- utilities (if not included in the common expenses);

- telephone, cable and Internet access (if not included in common expenses);
- amenity fees such as storage and parking (if you don't purchase your own parking spot or locker, or they are not included in common expenses); and
- maintenance costs of your individual unit.

RUNNING THE NUMBERS

So we've established the fact that there are a lot of issues to consider before buying a condo. How about we run some numbers through the House Rent versus Buy Analyzer to see what comes up? In this case I have assumed this is a condo that the purchaser will live in—not a rental unit.

To create a sample situation, I figured I'd drop into a new condo development in Toronto to gather actual sales literature and pricing information. This was not hard to do as there are dozens of them within a 10-minute drive of my house. I went into the presentation office of a condominium development to hear the pitch and, I must admit, it was impressive.

Since the development had not yet been built, the first order of business was a trip through a model one-bedroom suite. Very nice: ceramic tile flooring in the kitchen and laundry rooms, custom-designed cabinets with glass inserts, stainless steel sink and appliances, granite counter tops, built-in cook top, combination microwave and hood fan in the kitchen, stacked washer and dryer, marble counter top in the bathroom, and a decent-sized balcony to top it off.

The next step was a review of a 3-D artist's rendering of the development on a large wall-mounted high-definition TV hooked up to a computer. Here I saw the impressive two-storey front entrance lobby with 24-hour concierge, the elegant courtyard and the rooftop recreational facility, including outdoor lounge, dining area with five barbeques, the infinity-edge swimming pool, the party room, the games and fitness rooms, his and hers steam rooms and the private cabanas with their own barbeques and indoor and outdoor seating areas. It looked like a great place to live even though it did not exist yet!

The actual construction was to begin in late spring of 2012 with a projected move-in date of fall 2013. If I were to invest in a condo, it would be a one-bedroom so that's what I focused on. At this time there were only two left—the building was close to being sold out.

Here were the numbers for a one-bedroom with a den that was on the second floor with a total space of 751 square feet (710 square feet of interior space). Note that all prices included HST:

Price: $319,900
Maintenance: Approximately $0.45 per square foot
                    ($338 a month or $4,056 per year)
Hydro: Separately metered
Property taxes: Estimated at 0.83% of the purchase price ($2,655)
Parking spot: $18,000
Locker: $4,500

The required deposits were $2,500 on signing, then the balance to get up to 5% within 30 days, then another 5% within 120 days, another 5% within 180 days and another 5% on occupancy.

So, for the $319,900 one-bedroom that would be $2,500 upon signing, $13,495 within 30 days, $15,995 within four months, another $15,995 within six months and the remaining $15,995 upon moving in. The total deposit required came to $63,980, which is 20% of the purchase price. So in this case mortgage loan insurance would not be required.

The Toronto Condo: Results

I entered all the above information in the House Rent versus Buy Analyzer and made the following assumptions:

Rent

- The monthly rental costs for the unit would be $1,000 and they would increase at 1% per year;
- A last month's rent deposit of $1,000 would be required;
- Hydro costs that are separately metered would be $50 a month and increase at 2% per year;
- Two people would live in the condo and they have $40,000 of TFSA room available at the start with another $10,000 available each new year;

- The TFSA investments would grow at an annual rate of 3% per year after fees and the regular investment account would grow at an annual rate of 2.5% per year after fees and taxes;
- They also have $80,000 of unused RRSP deduction room and would add another $36,000 ($18,000 each) of RRSP deduction room each year;
- The RRSP investments would also grow at an annual rate of 3% per year after any fees;
- The couple's average marginal tax rate is 40% at the start as well as in 25 years when they sell the condo.

Buy

- $1,000 of closing costs for legal fees, etc.;
- The down payments totalling $63,980 represent 20% of the purchase price and therefore no mortgage loan insurance is required;
- The annual mortgage interest rate is 4% and the payments are made and compounded monthly;
- The mortgage is amortized over 25 years;
- The value of the condo will grow at 2% per year;
- The real estate commission on the sale of the condo after 25 years will be 5.0% of the selling price;
- Annual property taxes are $2,655 in the first year;
- Annual condominium fees are $4,056 in the first year;
- Hydro costs will be $600 in the first year (the same as the rental assumption);
- Annual insurance premiums on the unit are $800 in the first year;
- Property taxes, condominium fees, hydro costs and insurance premiums will increase at 2% per year;
- A parking spot is not required.

The chart on the following page shows the results for the TFSA option. Note that I have changed some of the wording in the spreadsheet; you should feel free to change the terminology in your own spreadsheet to suit your situation.

	Year	2012	2021	2031	2036
	Year #	1	10	20	25
RENT					
Rent Costs:					
Down payment		1,000			(1,000)
Rental payments		12,000	13,124	14,498	15,237
Heat, hydro		600	717	874	965
Total Rent Costs (A)		13,600	13,841	15,372	15,202
RENT Values					
TFSA					
Opening		0	143,783	311,310	415,576
Contribution		40,000	10,000	10,000	10,000
Growth (tax free)		1,200	4,613	9,639	12,767
Closing		41,200	158,396	330,949	438,343
INVESTMENT ACCOUNT					
Opening		0	61,992	106,439	135,868
Contribution		35,765	2,124	2,717	4,115
Growth (after tax)		894	1,603	2,729	3,500
Closing		36,659	65,719	111,885	143,483
TOTAL TFSA and Investment Account (C)		77,859	224,115	442,834	581,826
BUY					
Buy Costs:					
Down payment		63,980			
Closing costs		1,000			
Principal payments		6,108	8,749	13,044	15,926
Interest payments		10,166	7,524	3,230	347
Property taxes		2,655	3,172	3,866	4,268
Insurance		800	956	1,166	1,287
Condo fees		4,056	4,847	5,909	6,524
Heating (Oil or gas)		0	0	0	0
Electricity (Hydro)		600	717	874	965
Total Buy Costs (B)		89,365	25,965	28,089	29,317
ANNUAL EXCESS COSTS OF BUY (A-B)		(75,765)	(12,124)	(12,717)	(14,115)
BUY Values					
CONDO VALUE					
Opening		319,900	382,309	466,032	514,537
Growth		6,398	7,646	9,321	10,291
Closing		326,298	389,955	475,353	524,828
Mortgage balance		250,812	183,337	73,636	0
EQUITY IN CONDO (D)		75,486	206,618	401,717	524,828
EXCESS (DEFICIENT) VALUE EQUITY IN CONDO (D-C)		(2,373)	(17,497)	(41,117)	(56,998)
Proceeds on sale of condo					524,828
Real estate commission on sale					26,241
Net proceeds from sale of condo					498,587
EXCESS (DEFICENT) CASH ON SALE OF CONDO					(83,239)

At the end of 25 years, the condo renters would have $438,343 in their TFSAs and $143,483 in their regular investment accounts for a total of $581,826.

The condo is projected to be worth $524,828 after 25 years. After real estate commissions to sell of $26,241 (at 5.0%), the owners would be left with $498,587.

So the TFSA option yields $83,239 more than the buyers.

The RRSP results show that the renters would build up combined RRSP values of $958,306 and nothing in their regular investment accounts after 25 years. That is because in this example, the RRSP deduction room the couple had at the start and the deduction room they create each year, are sufficient to absorb all the excess cash they would have after each year and so there would be no regular investments outside of their RRSP.

If they then cashed in the RRSPs they would have to pay $383,322 in income tax (at 40%) and would be left with $574,984 cash in hand.

The RRSP option therefore yields $76,397 more than the buy option.

Playing with the Inputs

How would the outcome change if we made some different assumptions? Let's try some.

Condo Selling Price

What if we assume the value of the condo increased at a lower annual rate—say, 1% per year instead of 2%? All other inputs remaining equal, the TFSA option wins by $192,088 over the buy option and the RRSP option is projected to leave the renters with $185,246 more than the condo buyers.

Interest Rates

What if, over the next 25 years, interest rates average 2% per year higher than the original prediction? If we increase the assumed interest rate on the condo mortgage from 4% to 6%, the assumed annual increase on the TFSA and RRSP investments from 3% to 5% and the regular investments from 2.5% per year to 4.5% per year, we get some significant numbers.

If we go back to a 2% annual increase in the value of the condo, the buyers still end up with $498,587 after selling the condo.

The TFSA option shows the ending value of the TFSA and regular investment account to be $976,390 ($602,721 for the TFSA and $373,669 for the regular investments). That is $477,803 more than the buy option.

The RRSP option projects the RRSP to rise to $1,611,848 after 25 years. After cashing in and paying tax at 40% that would leave an estimated $967,109. That is $468,522 more than the buy option.

Again, I am not saying this will happen. Download the spreadsheet and enter your own assumptions.

Marginal Tax Rates

Let's change the marginal tax rates to see what the effect is on the results. This should only affect the TFSA and the RRSP options because marginal tax rates do not factor into the buy option, since we are assuming this is a principal residence and therefore there is no tax to pay on any eventual sale.

If we go back to the original scenario (2% per year increase in the condo price, mortgage loan rate of 4% per annum, TFSA/RRSP and investment account rates of 3% and 2.5% respectively), but assume the couple's marginal tax rate is 40% now but declines to 30% after 25 years (because they will be retired and living on less), the RRSP option results in $670,814 after-tax cash. This is $172,227 more than the buy option instead of $76,397 since there is $95,830 less tax owing when they cash in their RRSPs.

Further Analysis Required

Remember that this is just an example. It's not my opinion that renting a condo is always the better option. Your situation will most certainly be different—the spreadsheet may indicate buying is the better option. And of course if this is an investment rental property, you'll have to consider capital gains tax on the eventual sale as well as the ongoing rental income and expenses that need to be declared on your income tax return each year.

Every time I discuss the power of using a spreadsheet, I always warn users that it is just a tool that helps determine the outcome using different assumptions. It is great at doing this, but no matter how many variations you come up with, there are often factors that need to be considered that might render your spreadsheet predictions inaccurate. In a worst-case scenario, the real life numbers that actually happen could be significantly different.

For example, have you thought about real-life issues such as the loss of income after a child is born, especially if one or both parents is self-employed? This could significantly affect your ability to continue making maximum contributions to your RRSPs or TFSAs. As I have said, children are cash piglets, costing us a lot in terms of cash outflows but also in the reduction of cash inflows from lost income.

There are also issues that could occur that have nothing to do with the numbers. I always warn people that after going over the detailed financial issues it is absolutely vital to step back and think about the non-financial issues. In some cases, these issues are so significant that they over-ride the decision based solely on the numbers. Condominiums are no exception.

For example, say you buy your condo but have the misfortune of ending up with a unit beside a couple of obnoxious individuals that you can't stand. What do you do then? Even if your investment seems to be a good financial decision in the long run, who wants to live like that?

How are you going to deal with that risk? Well, before you buy you might try renting the unit for a few months if possible to get a sense of what your neighbours are like and how the building is operated. This would obviously not be possible with a condo that is not yet built, adding to the risk of a new purchase.

And there are many more risks, both financial and non-financial, associated with new and resale condos.

Buying a New Condominium

The CMHC *Condominium Buyers' Guide* lists the following advantages and disadvantages:

Advantages
- Possibly a lower purchase price depending on market conditions;
- More choice of locations within the building (especially if you get in early);
- A broad range of options and upgrades;
- Newer buildings have lower risk of needing costly, noisy and intrusive repairs and maintenance;
- New home warranty programs may be available.

Disadvantages

- You can't see and touch what you are buying and have to rely on artists' sketches and floor plans that may change (make sure you have the unit's location, boundaries, finishes, materials, chattels, etc., clearly specified in the purchase agreement);
- Your initial deposit will be tied up for the construction period, possibly earning no interest (note that also depends on market conditions—I recently saw a condo advertising 8% interest on deposits);
- Financial institutions may not give you a mortgage on an unregistered condominium;
- Construction on your unit may be delayed;
- Construction on other units may continue after you move into your unit, which can be noisy and disruptive.

Buying a Re-sale Condominium

The CMHC guide makes an important point here: when making an offer, always make it conditional on obtaining and having time to review the corporation documents that should be made available according to provincial legislation. This should include an estoppel or status certificate, the governing documents, financial statements and insurance coverage.

You should also consider hiring a qualified home inspector to conduct an inspection, and consider making the purchase contingent on it being successful. The last thing you want is to buy a condo and only find out afterward that it needs major, costly repairs.

Advantages

- You can see what you are buying;
- You can often move in sooner;
- Deposits are often much lower;
- There is no GST or HST on re-sale purchases;
- You can find out the types of people you will be living with and running the corporation;
- Older condominiums often have larger unit sizes.

Disadvantages

- Fewer options regarding choices of units and upgrades;
- Older buildings may require more repairs and maintenance;
- Amenities such as fitness rooms and 24-hour security may not be available;
- Older units may not be as energy efficient as newer ones;
- Major repairs may be looming with extra charges to unit owners if the reserve fund is not large enough to cover them;
- Any new home warranties may have expired.

CONDOS: WHAT COULD GO WRONG?

I must admit I have little real-life experience with condominiums so I decided to seek the advice of someone who has more knowledge than I do in the area. Kurt Rosentreter is a chartered accountant, investment advisor and insurance agent with Manulife Securities. He produces thought-provoking newsletters on financial strategies that are available for free at his website (www.kurtismycfo.com).

One he wrote dated September 2009 was titled "There is More to Condos than a Beautiful View." It is well worth the read and garnered a significant amount of media attention when it was released due to its hard-hitting style.

Kurt says that in his opinion "too many Canadians are being seduced by the pretty pictures and stories of easy lifestyle and they end up buying into a building that is a time bomb of costs that could render this lifestyle unaffordable over time."

He poses the question to condo owners and potential condo owners: "Do you really know what you are buying?"

Now to be fair, Kurt does not sell condominiums, he is an investment advisor and obviously has a vested interest in having clients invest their money in RRSPs, TFSAs and regular investment accounts rather than real estate, but he is one of the most knowledgeable people I have ever met when it comes to financial matters.

Having said that, this particular newsletter is a must-read if you are considering making a condo purchase because it details what could go wrong.

His first warning under the title "Big Picture Condo Economics" is to consider what you are buying when you purchase a condo unit. It is not just your unit. "You, and 300 strangers you want to have nothing to do with, are co-purchasing an $80 million+ building and all the maintenance costs associated with running it—forever."

That is a mighty big purchase to contemplate, especially if you are a retiree on a fixed pension or a young professional trying to make ends meet.

Here are a few of the highlights from the newsletter as to what can go wrong with a condo purchase:

- **Downsizing.** Selling your home in your sixties or seventies and moving to a condo to simplify your life may sound like a good idea, but in many cases, especially in big cities such as Toronto and Vancouver, it could actually end up costing more. The purchase price may be lower than what you get for your home, but higher property taxes and high condo fees could take a big chunk out of your living costs each year.
- **Monthly condo fees.** They may be lower in the beginning, especially for new condos, but the key is: how much will they increase by? The newsletter tells the story of one woman whose condo maintenance fees rose 15% per year over a five-year period to $900 a month. She concluded that she would be better off selling the condo, renting a suite for $900 a month, pocketing the original investment and getting away from the property taxes and condo fees.
- **Older condo risks.** As previously mentioned, there will usually be a contribution to the "reserve fund" included in your monthly maintenance fee. This is the money put aside for major repairs and maintenance by the condo corporation. But what if it's not big enough? The newsletter relates the story of an individual who received a one-time assessment of $12,500 as her share of the cost to fix a major crack in the underground parking ceiling. Fortunately she had the money, but what about those on a fixed pension or those without any savings? To put it mildly, this would put excessive pressure on the cash outflows: what else in your

budget could you cut to pay for something of that magnitude? It's a major risk that you can't do much to prevent.

- **The board of directors.** The condo board usually consists of residents who volunteer to manage the property's finances. They also hire and monitor the law firm that provides advice on all legal matters relating to the ownership and running of the property, the property management firm that carries out the daily duties of running the building, the bookkeeper and the external accounting firm that audits, or verifies, the accounting records. That is a large responsibility requiring a lot of time and a certain amount of expertise. It is often difficult finding people with the right mix of expertise, experience and time to run the condo corporation effectively.

What You Can Do to Manage Condo Risk

Just because there is risk that things can go wrong does not mean all is lost. Here are a few things that you should consider if you are a condo owner or thinking of becoming one:

Get Involved with the Board of Directors

Consider joining the board of directors of your condo and encouraging other owners to get involved. An inexperienced board can lead to major problems such as lack of sufficient control and monitoring of the property management company.

This point has unfortunately been illustrated recently in Toronto, where a condo property manager allegedly borrowed $20 million (perhaps even more) against nine condos that his company managed by forging signatures and creating false board of directors meeting minutes to register bylaws that allowed him to obtain the loans without the boards' knowledge. The property manager has apparently left the country and the condo owners are left with a significant liability.

Hire a Professional Property Management Firm

Be wary of a condo corporation that tries to save money by managing the property on its own. It is usually a huge job with potentially millions of dollars at stake. Assuming there is a property manager, make sure you monitor his or her actions on a continuous basis.

Monitor the Reserve Fund Study

Make sure that an authorized independent professional firm has been engaged to perform a detailed study regarding the size of the reserve fund and that it is updated regularly to ensure that the monthly maintenance fees are building up enough money to avoid significant special assessments down the road.

Read the Minutes of the Annual General Meeting

Do this before you buy to determine how the owners get along. Were there many disputes and problems or did it go smoothly? Be very careful if there has not been an annual general meeting in the last year as required.

If you already are an owner, make sure you attend each of these meetings to voice any concerns you may have and to find out about any other issues that may affect you and your investment.

Review the Annual Audited Financial Statements

This document tells you where all the money went as well as the state of the assets, liabilities and commitments of the condo corporation as certified by an independent professional accountant. If you aren't good with numbers, get a friendly accountant to have a look and give you his or her honest opinion about what is going on.

A Word about Rental Properties and Income Tax

If you are considering purchasing a condominium as a rental property there are extra tax issues you have to be aware of.

First of all, if you sell the rental property at a later date for more than you purchased it for, the resulting profit, called a capital gain, is taxable. In Canada, 50% of the capital gain needs to be reported as income on the income tax return of the seller and is then taxed at his or her marginal tax rate. This could be as high as 46% in

Ontario, for example. (Again, as most people know, any gain on the sale of a principal residence—the home where you live—is not taxable in Canada.)

But there is another tax issue with respect to rental investments that you should be aware of. Kurt Rosentreter points this out in his newsletter: "Canada Revenue Agency (CRA) has made it clear in recent years that if you purchase a rental property you need to have a business plan to generate profit over time. In the past, landlords thought it brilliant to claim rental losses year after year and deduct these losses against their regular income, reducing their tax bill."

Not anymore. Many condo owner landlords have faced audits by CRA that led to disallowed losses, sometimes going back several years, as CRA has forced taxpayers to prove they have a valid business. Many can't make that claim.

Here is an example from the newsletter to illustrate the point:

Purchase price of the condo: $400,000
Mortgage at 6% annual interest: $350,000
First-year interest costs: $21,000 ($350,000 × 6%)
Gross rental income: $19,200 ($1,600 × 12 months)

In this example, the interest expense exceeds the rental income. There is a rental loss even before considering property taxes, maintenance fees, utilities, insurance or any other costs of renting out the condo.

In CRA's view it is pretty difficult to see how this condo will be profitable any time soon. And that is important to them—why should they allow you to write off losses and reduce your tax bill when there is little hope for them ever to collect any tax on income?

Rosentreter concludes that unless you are putting down a major deposit leading to a small mortgage, it is not advisable to try to claim the losses on your tax return.

CONDO WRAP-UP

There is no doubt a condominium is a cash pig. They are pigs in the short term due to the cash demands to purchase and maintain them. Like a house on a desirable plot of land, however, there may be a jackpot at the end. You could sell for more than you originally paid for it, but there is no guarantee. If the condo market in your area loses value, you could be stuck with a unit that no longer meets your needs and no one willing to pay a good price to take it off your hands.

Remember the old adage about real estate: they aren't making any more of it. Well, when it comes to condos, they are. In some areas they are making many more of them. That makes it a much more risky proposition than buying a house. That's because the house is on land—and they're not making any more of that.

When it comes to condos, it is buyer beware—especially these days.

7

INFLATION: MONSTER OR MYTH?

When monitoring our cash flow we need to consider how inflation will affect our cash inflows and outflows going forward. Inflation has the potential to be a real cash pig in the future and could become a major problem for people when it comes to the outflows—their expenses. Unfortunately, inflation is one cash pig that we can't do much about. The environment in which we live will determine where inflation is going in the future, and there's nothing you can do to stop it, or even predict it.

But that doesn't mean we should give up and ignore it.

Before we try to go to battle with the mythical inflation monster, let's try to understand what it's all about.

WHAT IS INFLATION?

Dictionary.com defines inflation as:

A persistent, substantial rise in the general level of prices related to an increase in the volume of money and resulting in the loss of value of currency.

Inflation simply means that the price of goods and services is rising. If, for example, we bought a bottle of water for $1 on January 1 and a year later that same bottle cost $1.02 that would be a 2% rate of inflation.

It also means that the purchasing power of $1 is declining since the same dollar can't buy the same bottle of water a year from now.

It results in increasing cash outflows—with no additional benefit to us. Things just cost more and there is not much you can do about it. As we'll see later in this chapter, this can have a significant impact on what your cash flow looks like in the years to come.

THE CONSUMER PRICE INDEX (CPI)

In Canada, the CPI is the most widely used measure of inflation. This index tracks the cost of a fixed basket of over 600 separate consumer goods and services over a period of time. The items in the basket are adjusted to maintain consistent quantities and qualities so the index reflects only price movements.

Statistics Canada (www.statcan.gc.ca) is the government entity that tracks the CPI.

The CPI is important to Canadians because it is used to adjust things like the Old Age Security (OAS) pensions, the Canada Pension Plan (CPP) premiums and payments, as well as other social and welfare payments.

It is also used to set price increases in rental agreements, spousal and child support payments and cost-of-living adjustment (COLA) clauses in many labour contracts of Canadian workers.

The goods and services in the CPI basket are those considered to be consumer items. They include goods from ground beef to spark plugs, and services from haircuts to property taxes.

The prices used in the index are the retail prices that a consumer would have to pay to purchase the good or service. Note that no attempt is made to distinguish between luxuries and necessities and that nothing is omitted based on moral or social judgement; items such as tobacco and alcohol are included because Canadians spend money on these things even though they are not necessities and some people find them socially undesirable.

The items in the basket are organized into a classification system. Items are grouped with similar items into "basic classes." There are about 182 basic classes in all. These basic classes are then combined into larger groups. The highest level before the "All-items" index is the "major component." There are eight major components in the All-items index, as follows:

1. Food
2. Shelter
3. Household operations, furnishings and equipment
4. Clothing and footwear
5. Transportation
6. Health and personal care
7. Recreation, education and reading
8. Alcoholic beverages and tobacco products

Indexes are calculated for all basic classes.

It is important to note that there is more than one CPI figure. The most common one is the "All-items" index. This includes all major classes and therefore all items in the index. Categories can be combined to meet specific needs. Common examples include the "All-items excluding food" and "All-items excluding energy" indexes, which some economists believe are better measures of underlying trends in price changes than the All-items index.

Other well-known combinations include "Goods," "Services," "Energy" and "All-items excluding tobacco products."

Tables are also created for each province and territory and for 33 separate metropolitan areas.

How the CPI Is Calculated
Weighting

First of all the relative importance of each item, or basic class, is determined. The spending on each item is compared to total spending in Canada to get the relative importance, or weight, of each item. Weights determine the impact that a price change of a particular item will have on the overall index.

For example, a 5% increase in the price of milk will have a higher weighting than a 5% rise in the price of tea because Canadians drink more milk than tea. The weight assigned to milk (0.69%) is therefore higher than tea (0.06%).

The content and weighting of the items in the CPI basket are reviewed and updated periodically to ensure it reflects changes in spending patterns due to changes in things like the composition and distribution of the population, the quality and availability of goods and services, personal incomes and consumer taste.

Collecting Prices

Prices are constantly being updated through surveys that determine the price a consumer would have to pay on a particular day. If that day happens to have a sale on the item, the sale price is used. Since sales taxes such as GST and HST are part of the price paid by the consumer, they are included in the final price used in the CPI index.

Most items are priced once per month. Some items are priced less frequently because their prices don't tend to change as often. For example, haircuts and dry-cleaning services are only priced each quarter and property taxes and tuition fees only once a year.

More than 60,000 price quotations are collected each month by trained interviewers based in the regional offices of Statistics Canada. To ensure that price movements reflect the experience of most of the population, they track the most popular brands.

Adjusting for Quality Changes

It is important to note that Statistics Canada tries to discount price increases due to improvements in the products since they are tracking only price changes. One way they do this is to determine what feature of a product caused the price to change and adjust the old cost for that feature. For example, when air conditioning became a standard feature in newer model cars, they estimated the cost of the air conditioning and added that to the price of the older vehicle that did not have that option.

Calculating the Indexes

Once the price data is gathered, it is then scrutinized and the particular weighting of each basic element is applied. Various basic elements are combined to produce group indexes. For example, the price indexes for milk, butter, cheese and other dairy products are combined to form the index for dairy products. Then these groups are further combined to form the eight major component indexes and they are combined to form the All-items index.

The CPI Time Base

The time base or base period is the period, usually a specific year, in which the index is assigned a value of 100. The CPI base year is currently 2002. It is important whenever a value is given that the base year is also disclosed. For example, the CPI All-items index for 2011 was 119.9 (2002 = 100). That means that prices overall were 19.9% higher in 2011 than they were in 2002.

To calculate the percentage price change between two periods you don't subtract one from the other. Instead, you divide the more recent index by the older index, multiply by 100, and then subtract 100.

For example, the CPI All-items index was 119.9 in 2011 and 116.5 in 2010. The percentage change in overall prices was therefore 2.9% calculated as follows:

- $((119.9/116.5) \times 100) - 100 = 2.9\%$

Historical CPI Rates

So what does the CPI tell us about price changes in Canada recently? Let's have a look.

The following is a table of historical CPI figures for 2011 with a base year of 2002 = 100 in the left column and the % change from the previous year in the right column:[1]

Consumer Price Index, Canada, 2011

	Value, 2002 = 100	% Change from Previous yr.
All-items	119.9	2.9
Food	127.7	3.7
Shelter	125.6	1.9

[1] http://www.statcan.gc.ca/tables-tableaux/sum-som/l01/cst01/econ09a-eng.htm

Household operations, furnishings and equipment	110.9	1.9
Clothing and footwear	91.9	0.3
Transportation	125.6	6.4
Health and personal care	117.1	1.7
Recreation, education and reading	105.3	1.3
Alcoholic beverages and tobacco products	135.6	1.9
Special aggregates		
All-items excluding food	118.3	2.8
All-items excluding energy	117.0	1.9

We can see that overall prices have risen by 2.9% since 2010 with the highest rate of increase in the transportation category at 6.4% and the lowest increase in clothing and footwear at 0.3%.

This is useful information for determining Canada-wide policy like CPP and OAS rates, but what about us as individuals? Say you live in Alberta and are interested in prices in your province.

Here is the same table for the Province of Alberta:[2]

Consumer Price Index, Alberta, 2011		
	Value, 2002 = 100	**% Change from Previous yr.**
All-items	125.7	2.4
Food	125.6	3.1
Shelter	152.1	3.0
Household operations, furnishings and equipment	109.2	1.4

[2] http://www.statcan.gc.ca/tables-tableaux/sum-som/l01/cst01/econ09j-eng.htm

Consumer Price Index, Alberta, 2011 (*Continued*)		
	Value, 2002 = 100	**% Change from Previous yr.**
Clothing and footwear	93.9	(2.2)
Transportation	124.7	5.0
Health and personal care	124.7	2.7
Recreation, education and reading	105.7	(0.3)
Alcoholic beverages and tobacco products	135.0	1.0
Special aggregates		
All-items excluding food	125.7	2.3
All-items excluding energy	122.4	1.2

As you can see, by drilling down to the provincial level, we have much more relevant information. For example, it seems that the cost of shelter has risen more dramatically in Alberta than the whole of Canada—by 3.0% since the previous year versus only 1.9% for all of Canada.

Two categories—clothing and footwear, as well as recreation, education and reading—have both had declining prices since the previous year by −2.2% and −0.3% respectively. In Canada overall, both those categories increased in price. If either of these categories were important to you because you spent money on them in Alberta, basing your spending projections on the Alberta table would yield a more accurate result.

Of course there is no guarantee that the ratios will continue the next year, but it's the best information we can get to at least make an educated guess.

Percentages versus Actual Cash Flow

At this point I'd like to get you to think about just what a percentage increase means.

It is the amount by which an item's cost rises in a year, compared to what it cost at the beginning of the year. Focusing on the percentage change, however, can be very misleading.

For example, say you spend $3 on a tube of toothpaste and you used 10 tubes during 2010. That category therefore cost you $30 in 2010.

Another item—gas for your car—cost you $75 per fill-up and you filled up your car three times a month in 2010 for a total cost of $2,700.

If both items rose in price by 5%, the cost of all your toothpaste in 2011 (assuming you used the same quantity and quality) would rise by $1.50 to $31.50 ($30 × 1.05) from $30.

Your gas costs for 2011 would have risen by $135 to $2,835 ($2,700 × 1.05). The same percentage increase has a much more significant effect on your pocketbook.

If you just focus on the percentage increase, you could end up spending time worrying about things that are small and therefore not that important.

Because of this I find it helpful to translate percentages to actual dollars whenever possible.

An Inflation Example

The following table summarizes the average expenditures for Canadian households in 2009 according to Statistics Canada:

Average expenditures by Canadian household, 2009	
	Amount
Food	$7,262
Shelter	$14,095
Household operation	$3,428
Household furnishings and equipment	$1,896
Clothing	$2,841
Transportation	$9,753
Health care	$2,004

Average expenditures by Canadian household, 2009 (*Continued*)	Amount
Personal care	$1,200
Recreation	$3,843
Reading materials and other printed matter	$232
Education	$1,238
Tobacco products and alcoholic beverages	$1,506
Games of chance (net)	$255
Miscellaneous expenditures	$1,181
Personal taxes	$14,399
Personal insurance payments and pension contributions	$4,269
Gifts of money and contributions	$1,715
Total	$71,117

Applying the CPI All-items index rate of 2.9% to the total expenditures of $71,117 would imply that the next year they would increase by $2,062—2.9% of $71,117. But that would be misleading.

The first thing we need to realize is that some of the expenditures listed are not affected by inflation. Personal taxes of $14,399 in this case will not go up by inflation. They may go up or down depending on the taxable income of the people involved.

There are also several discretionary expenditures like household furnishings and equipment, recreation, reading materials and other printed matter, tobacco products and alcoholic beverages, games of chance, miscellaneous expenditures and gifts of money and contributions. In this case these total $10,628. Since we have a lot of control over how much we spend on these things, we are not really held hostage if their costs increase. We could choose to spend less in these categories and keep the amounts the same or even decrease them.

So combined with personal taxes, the total amount not really impacted by inflation comes to $25,027—35% of the total expenditures.

Where inflation is really going to impact the average Canadian family is in the basic necessities of life—food, shelter, household operations, clothing, transportation, health care and education.

For example, using the CPI All-items index rates of 3.7% for food and 1.9% for shelter for 2011, in this case food costs are projected to increase by $268 to $7,530 and shelter costs are projected to increase by $268 to $14,363 over the next year. That illustrates the importance of focusing on the actual expenses rather than just the percentages. Food is increasing at a greater rate but is a lower amount of actual dollars than shelter is to begin with. So even though shelter costs are rising more slowly the impact on the pocketbook is the same. They are equal cash pigs in this case.

We each need to consider where our money is going by category; then and only then will we be able to project how inflation is going to affect each of our spending lines, and therefore our pocketbooks, going forward.

Where Will Inflation Be in the Future?

But the CPI is a historical index. It tracks price increases in the past. What is really important to us is prices in the future, and unfortunately Statistics Canada can't predict the future.

Even if we track our own spending and go through it line by line, as we just did, that will give us useful information, but only if past rates continue going forward.

But what is going to happen next? How worried do we all need to be about future rising prices? There is no right answer but that doesn't mean we can't make an educated guess.

I'm going to make a stab here using basic logic, not any complex macro-economic theory.

It would seem to me that there will definitely be rising prices going forward especially for certain items like gasoline. We have already seen this happening and with a resource that is being depleted every day, the lack of supply usually means rising prices ahead. What can you do about that? Well, you could drive less and switch to public transit or carpool and these are choices that people will likely start to make, especially those on limited budgets and those who have decided to stop using increasing debt balances to spend more than they make.

The good news is some prices will actually decrease. Computer prices, for example, have been dropping like stones over recent years: I do my presentations on a netbook computer that cost $299. Several years ago I used a notebook computer that cost me in excess of $3,000. That is deflation, not inflation.

But deflation is not necessarily a good thing.

Deflation May Be the Bigger Monster

While declining prices may benefit us as individuals, since it costs us less to get what we need, on a larger scale it can be catastrophic.

Investopedia.com defines deflation as follows:

> *A general decline in prices, often caused by a reduction in the supply of money or credit. Deflation can be caused also by a decrease in government, personal or investment spending. The opposite of inflation, deflation has the side effect of increased unemployment since there is a lower level of demand in the economy, which can lead to an economic depression. Central banks attempt to stop severe deflation, along with severe inflation, in an attempt to keep the excessive drop in prices to a minimum.*[3]

While politicians and finance officials do not often talk about deflation in public, I am sure they are worried about it in private. That is because persistent declining prices can create a vicious cycle of declining corporate profits, shrinking employment and income, factory closings and loan defaults by corporations and individuals.

The Bank of Canada can try to stop deflation from happening by causing inflation. The main tool they use to do this is reducing interest rates, which makes it cheaper for businesses and individuals to borrow money. The key rate the Bank of Canada uses is the Overnight Rate, which is currently 1%. So they have only a bit of room to reduce rates.

---

[3]http://www.investopedia.com/search/default.aspx?q = deflation#axzz21BprObSX

The problem is that this doesn't always work. Japan, for example, has had several decades of deflation that started in the early 1990s, even though the government there reduced interest rates to zero.

If deflation rears its ugly head, we will all be hoping for inflation because rising prices mean increased profits for businesses, which usually translates to more employment for individuals and higher corporate and personal income taxes for the government. You may not like paying personal income taxes (or corporate taxes, for those who are business owners) but paying tax is in fact a sign of a healthy economy. We can't expect to live in a great country if the government does not receive the income tax revenues needed to finance its operations.

Stagflation: The Two-Headed Beast

One of the worst possible situations to be in is a period of stagflation. That is a slow economic growth, high unemployment and rising prices. It is basically deflation and inflation at the same time and it is horrible.

This is what it is like in countries such as Greece today. The European leaders are doing all they can to try to turn the tide, but it is one of the most complex economic problems that exists.

Whew, that was a depressing section to write. Let's move on.

WHY THE CPI MATTERS TO YOU

As we have seen, the CPI is the common measure of inflation but relying on it may lead us astray. That is because the CPI is just an average of a huge basket of consumer goods, some of which may not be part of your spending pattern.

What is important to each of us is our personal CPI. Determining your personal CPI starts with knowing where your money has gone in the past. Resolve to find out. That means you'll need to sit down with your bank statements and credit card bills for at least the past month and preferably for the past year. Add up each major category: housing costs broken down by mortgage payments, repairs and maintenance, heat, hydro, insurance, etc. Break down automobile costs by loan/lease payments, gas, repairs and maintenance, insurance, etc. Make a record of the cost of raising your cash piglets: daycare, camp, schooling, clothing, etc. You'll obviously have many more categories than these, but the key is to summarize them so you know where the cash pigs are.

Then and only then will you be able to identify what affect inflation is likely to have on your outflows. If you don't go through this exercise you are leaving your future cash flows to chance. Hoping that things will work out is not a good strategy. In fact, it is not a strategy at all. Staring your cash pigs in the face is the only way to get control of them. And you can't do that if you don't summarize them.

You then need to think about your future. What are the things that you'll be buying in the future? Are there categories that will disappear, such as some kid-related expenses?

It is possible that as you age you'll find that many spending categories are actually going to decline with time. That means certain cash outflows will become less significant and that even if inflation attacks the item, it will not affect you that much.

So there may be good news for you, but you won't know unless you start to track your own spending. Don't let your cash pigs get the better of you—take control today.

MAXIMIZING YOUR CANADA PENSION PLAN

As Canadians who are employed or self-employed we have no choice but to pay into the Canada Pension Plan. But the CPP is not a tax: we are paying into it so that we can receive money out of it after we stop working. It is a forced savings mechanism, and for many people that is a good thing because they don't have the discipline to do it themselves. The CPP is therefore a cash pig when we are working and a cash cow after we stop.

For many Canadians, the Canada Pension Plan will be a vital source of cash in retirement—a valuable component of the Cash Cow Strategy. But you need to know the new details to make sure you get what you deserve out of it.

What new details?

Well, the government has recently changed many of the rules concerning the Canada Pension Plan (CPP). These changes are already coming into effect. It has also proposed changes to the Old Age Security (OAS) pension in the federal budget of March 29, 2012, that have yet to be implemented. These changes are likely to have a significant impact on your retirement plans and your cash flow in retirement. This chapter and the next will give you the information you need.

CPP AND OAS OVERVIEW

The CPP is a government-guaranteed defined benefit pension plan that we pay into during our working years. When we retire it will pay us cash for life. The OAS pension is also paid for life once you start to receive it.

The difference between the two pension plans is that you don't pay into the OAS directly like you do with the CPP. Since the OAS is paid by the government out of its general income tax revenues, payments of the OAS pension show up as an expense on the federal government's income statement. Thus OAS payments increase the annual deficit. The CPP is different as it is accounted for separately.

These programs are administered by Service Canada, which has an excellent website that is well laid out and easy to navigate. For the latest information check it out at http://www.servicecanada.gc.ca/eng/home.shtml. I have also found the people I have talked to there to be very helpful. If you have specific questions about your situation that you can't find answers to on their website, their phone number is 1-800-277-9914.

Let's get into the details so you can make sure to maximize the amounts you get out of these plans.

CPP: The Basics

The Canada Pension Plan is a contributory, earnings-related social insurance program that provides an inflation-adjusted basic pension for the remainder of your life, once you become eligible to receive it. It also provides you and your dependents with basic financial protection if you become disabled or die. Here are the components.

- **Retirement Pension.** Provides a monthly taxable benefit to retired contributors.
- **Disability Benefits.** Provides a monthly taxable benefit to contributors who are disabled and to their dependent children.
- **Survivor's Pension.** Provides a monthly pension to the surviving spouse, common-law partner or children of a deceased contributor.

- **Children's Benefits.** Provides a monthly benefit to the dependent children of disabled or deceased contributors.
- **Death Benefit.** Provides a one-time payment of up to $2,500 to, or on behalf of, the estate of a deceased contributor.
- **International Benefits.** This program of the Canadian government provides social security benefits to eligible individuals who have lived or worked in another country, or to the surviving spouse or common-law partner of eligible individuals who have lived or worked in another country.

The CPP operates in all provinces and territories except Quebec, where the Quebec Pension Plan (QPP) provides benefits.

You qualify for the CPP pension if you worked and made at least one valid contribution to the CPP. The amount you receive will depend on how much you paid into it and for how many years.

The regular age to start receiving your CPP is 65 but you can elect to start receiving it as early as age 60 if you are willing to accept a penalty to do so.

The CPP pension does not start automatically. You must apply to start receiving it. You can print off, fill in and mail form ISP-1000 ("Application for Canada Pension Plan Retirement Pension"), which is available on the Service Canada website.

Alternatively, you can apply electronically on Service Canada's website at http://www.servicecanada.gc.ca/eng/isp/common/rtrinfo.shtml in two steps:

1. Complete and submit your application electronically to Service Canada.
2. Print and sign a signature page and mail it to Service Canada.

To use the on-line service you must have contributed to the CPP and be at least one day past the month following your 59th birthday. You must also want your retirement pension payments to begin within 11 months of the date you apply and have access to a computer that meets minimum requirements with JavaScript enabled.

Gather the following information before you begin:

- Your Social Insurance Number (SIN);
- If you wish to arrange for direct deposit of the funds, the financial institution number of your bank as well as the branch and account number;
- If you were the primary caregiver of any children or received Family Allowance or Child Tax Benefits while they were under the age of seven,
  - the SIN of each child; and,
  - the date of entry into Canada for each child born outside of Canada.
- If you want to take advantage of CPP pension sharing for possible tax savings, your spouse or common-law partner's SIN;
- If you lived or worked in a country other than Canada and want to apply for benefits from that country, details of when you worked or lived outside Canada and your SIN there.

Note that the on-line service is not available for individuals presently receiving a CPP (or QPP) disability benefit.

CPP: The New Rules

The government has recently made significant changes to the CPP. They were approved in Bill C-51, which was passed into law December 15, 2009, and came into effect beginning in 2011.

The only people not affected by these changes are those who started to receive their CPP pension before December 31, 2010, and who remain out of the workforce.

Here are the changes.

Penalty for Early Election

The penalty used to be 0.5% per month (6% per year) but is increasing to 0.6% per month (7.2% per year) from 2012 to 2016.

So starting to receive CPP payments at age 60 would have cost you 30% under the old rules (6% × 5 years) and will cost you 36% under the new rules (7.2% × 5 years).

For example, under the old rules if you started at age 60 you would get only 70% of what you would have received at age 65—that is, $70 for every $100 you would have received if you waited until age 65.

Under the new rules, in 2016 if you start at age 60 you will only get 64% of what you would have received at age 65—that is, $64 for every $100 you would have received if you waited until age 65.

Here is the schedule of increases to the penalty:

CPP Penalty for Early Election Rates			
Year	Per Month	Per Year	Maximum 5 Years
2012	0.52%	6.24%	31.2%
2013	0.54%	6.48%	32.4%
2014	0.56%	6.72%	33.6%
2015	0.58%	6.96%	34.8%
2016	0.60%	7.2%	36.0%

Bonus for Late Election

Under the old rules, you were paid a bonus of 0.5% per month to wait to receive your CPP pension for every month after your 65th birthday up until age 70. There is no financial benefit to delaying receiving your CPP pension after age 70.

Under the new rules this bonus will be increased to 0.64% per month in 2012 (7.68% per year) to 0.7% per month (8.4% per year) in 2013.

That means that in 2013 if you start to receive your CPP pension at age 70 you will receive 42% more than you would have at age 65 (8.4% × 5 years). That would be $142 instead of $100.

We'll discuss this important decision later in this chapter.

Elimination of Work Cessation Test

Up until 2011 if you elected to receive your Canada Pension early there was a work cessation test. This required you to stop working by the end of the month before your CPP began and during the month in which it began, or earn less than the maximum monthly retirement pension in those two months.

The work cessation test has been eliminated starting in 2012 so you can now start to receive your CPP pension as early as age 60 without having to stop working or reduce earnings.

Working While Receiving the CPP (Under 65)

In the past, if you elected to receive your Canada Pension before age 65 and then went back to work, you did not have to make any more CPP contributions.

Effective in 2012, if you are under 65 and you work while receiving your CPP pension, you and your employer will have to make mandatory CPP contributions. These funds will go toward the new "Post-Retirement Benefit" (PRB).

The PRB is a new lifetime benefit that increases your retirement income and rises with the cost of living even if you already draw the maximum CPP or QPP pension. Canadians working outside of Quebec who receive a CPP or QPP pension had to start making contributions to the PRB on January 1, 2012.

You don't have to apply for the PRB. If you made contributions toward your PRB, it will be paid to you automatically each year starting the year after you make the contributions. For example, if you were required to pay into your PRB in 2012, the resulting PRB benefit will be paid to you each year beginning in 2013. If you were required to pay into your PRB again in 2013, an additional amount of PRB benefit will be paid to you each year beginning in 2014. Additional information about the PRB including a table to estimate the amount you will receive based on your income is available at http://www.servicecanada.gc.ca/eng/isp/cpp/prb/index.shtml#b1.

Working While Receiving the CPP (65 to 70)

Starting in 2012, if you are at least 65 but under 70 and you work while receiving your CPP pension, you will be required to make CPP contributions that will go toward your PRB.

If you don't want to do this, you have to elect not to contribute.

For employees this is done by filling in a form and providing it to your employer. The form is available from the Canada Revenue Agency (CRA) website. It is form CPT30 ("Election to Stop Contributing to the Canada Pension Plan, or Revocation of a Prior Election").

If you are self-employed and at least age 65 but under 70, and wish to opt out of paying into your PRB, do not use form CPT30. Instead, complete the applicable section of Schedule 8 ("CPP Contributions on Self-Employment and Other Earnings") and file it with your Income Tax and Benefit Return for 2012 or any year after that. If you use a software package to file your taxes, Schedule 8 should automatically appear if it is applicable.

If you are both an employee and self-employed, at least 65 but under 70, and receiving a CPP or QPP pension, you can elect to stop contributing to the CPP by completing form CPT30 and giving it to your employer and sending the original to the Canada Revenue Agency. The election takes effect on the first day of the month following the date you give a copy of the form to your employer. If you do this, make sure you don't calculate and make CPP contributions on your self-employment earnings when you file your income tax return.

Increased General Drop-Out Provision Years

You don't have to contribute the maximum CPP contributions each and every year from your 18th birthday until age 65 to receive the maximum CPP pension.

When Service Canada calculates the amount of CPP pension a person is eligible to receive, they use the person's average earnings over his or her contributory period. This period is from the latest of January 1, 1966 (when the CPP started), or age 18 until the effective date of his or her retirement pension if effective before the age of 70. Under the old rules 15% of the lowest earnings were automatically dropped from the calculation. This is called the "general drop-out provision."

Under this provision, prior to 2012, up to 15% of the years of your lowest earnings would be dropped from the calculation of your average earnings. If you took your CPP pension at age 65, that would be seven years, which is 15% of the 47 years from age 18 to 65.

In 2012 and 2013 the percentage of low earnings years will increase to 16%, allowing up to 7.5 years of the lowest earnings years to be dropped from the calculation for people who begin receiving the pension at age 65. In 2014 the percentage will increase to 17% (8 years).

CPP Contribution Rate

The Canada Pension Plan is financed through mandatory contributions from employers, employees and self-employed individuals, as well as through revenue generated from the investments the plan holds.

The combined contribution rate is currently 9.9% of earnings between the Year's Basic Exemption of $3,500 and the Year's Maximum Pensionable Earnings, which is $50,100 in 2012. Employers and employees split the contribution rate equally so the maximum paid by each of them in 2012 is 4.95%.

Employers and employees therefore pay $2,306.70 ((50,100 − 3,500) × 4.95%) in 2012, whereas self-employed people pay $4,613.40 ((50,100 − 3,500) × 9.9%).

Is the CPP Plan Solid?

You may occasionally hear someone say that the Canada Pension Plan might not be able to pay out your CPP pension because the large number of people who will be retiring before you will drain its resources.

If that were the case, the CPP would be a real cash pig—draining our cash each and every year and then not paying us back in the end. But is that a significant risk?

Before we try to answer the question, we need to look back a few years at why some people might think this way.

CPP: 1996 Financial Challenges

In 1996 the CPP paid out $17 billion in benefits while receiving only $11 billion in contributions. An actuarial report at the time projected that the CPP's small contingency reserve would be exhausted by 2015. It went on to say that a contribution rate of 14% would be necessary by 2030, effectively meaning future generations would be forced to pay for the pensions of existing retirees.

The factors that caused this issue included:

- an aging population;
- a series of benefit enhancements;
- slow earnings growth of the CPP's investments;
- higher benefit payments for those with disabilities.

CPP Response to Financial Challenges

In February 1997 the federal government and the provinces reached agreement on major reforms to the CPP as follows:

- a modest reduction in future benefits;
- an increase in the contribution rates from 5.6% in 1996 to 9.9% in 2003 in order to create a larger reserve fund;
- the creation of an organization called the CPP Investment Board (CPPIB) to operate at arm's length from the governments and free from political interference. The CPPIB is responsible for managing the reserve fund to ensure future generations won't be saddled with paying for the pensions of previous generations.

These reforms included an amending formula that requires the federal government and two-thirds of the provinces (representing two-thirds of the population) to agree on any change to the plan, its contribution rate, benefits and any other fundamental issues.

The CPP Investment Board (CPPIB)

The CPPIB invests excess funds of the Canada Pension Plan not currently needed by the CPP to pay benefits. Its investment policy is to "maximize investment returns without undue risk of loss." It is a professional investment management organization with a disclosure policy that states, "Canadians have the right to know why, how and where we invest their Canadian Pension Plan money, who makes the investment decisions, what assets are owned on their behalf, and how the investments are performing."

They have a detailed website (www.cppib.ca) and are required to issue quarterly and annual financial statements and public disclosure of portfolio holdings.

To reduce the risk of political interference and ensure strong public accountability, the following is set out in the legislation that governs the CPPIB:

- The investment professionals of the CPPIB report to an independent board of directors;
- Directors are appointed by the federal finance minister in consultation with his counterparts in the participating provinces and assisted by an external nominating committee with private sector involvement;
- The board of directors hires the CEO, sets investment policies, reviews performance, approves external investment management partners, sets compensation for management that is linked to long-term performance and appoints independent auditors;
- A code of conduct compels members of the board of directors and management to report any attempted political influence of investment decisions.

The CPPIB Reserve Fund

How much money does the CPPIB have? It has a diverse portfolio of public and private equities (stocks), real estate, inflation-linked bonds, fixed income and infrastructure instruments.

At March 31, 2012, the total value of the fund was $161.6 billion. Here is how the investments were distributed:

- Foreign developed market equities   35.1%
- Bonds and money market securities   25.8%
- Canadian equities   8.8%
- Real estate   10.6%
- Other debt   5.4%
- Infrastructure   5.8%
- Emerging market equities   6.5%
- Inflation-linked bonds   2.0%
- Total   100.0%

Here is a summary of the CPPIB fund's value, asset growth, CPP net contributions, net investment income from operations and portfolio return for the last five years:[1]

CPPIB Annual Fiscal Year Summaries (Cdn $ billions)*					
	2008	**2009**	**2010**	**2011**	**2012**
Total Assets	122.7	105.5	127.6	148.2	161.6
Asset Growth	6.1	(17.2)	22.1	20.6	13.4
CPP Net Contributions	6.5	6.6	6.1	5.4	3.9
Net Investment Income from Operations	(0.4)	(23.8)	16.0	15.2	9.5
Portfolio Returns (%)	(0.3)	(18.6)	14.9	11.9	6.6

* All years are at the fiscal year-end of March 31.

For the five-year period ended March 31, 2012, the CPP fund generated an annualized rate of return of 2.2%, or $17.7 billion of cumulative investment income.

For the 10-year period the annualized return was 6.2%, or $59.4 billion of cumulative investment income.

So while not infallible, the CPPIB and its reserve fund seem to be well positioned to fulfill their mandate.

The Chief Actuary of Canada

The Chief Actuary of Canada is required to conduct a thorough review of the CPP every three years to ensure that it is achieving its objectives. In November 2010 the conclusion reached was that the CPP remains

---

[1] http://www.cppib.ca/Results/Financial_Highlights/

sustainable at the current contribution rate of 9.9% throughout the 75-year period of his report.

Contributions are expected to exceed annual benefits paid through until 2021 and there is no need to use current income to pay benefits for another 10 years.

Starting in 2021 the CPP fund is expected to continue to grow, but at a slower rate, as some of the investment income will be needed to help pay the pensions.

CAN WE COUNT ON THE CPP?

Let's review where we stand on the CPP.

We have already seen that the CPP has had its funding issues in the past and that the governments have stepped in to get it back on solid ground.

We have seen that the CPPIB, an independent, arm's-length body charged with ensuring that CPP funds earn a decent rate of return while avoiding undue risk, seems to be operating effectively.

We know that all employers, employees and self-employed individual people are required to pay into it.

We also know that the Chief Actuary of Canada reviews the CPP every three years to determine if the current contribution rate needs increasing. If it does, the government will increase it.

The next time you hear someone dismiss the CPP as something we can't count on, review all the preceding issues with them and ask them why.

It would seem to me a pretty safe bet that we can rely on the CPP cash cow after we retire—at least for the next 70 years.

Is the Canada Pension Plan a Good Investment?

Some people are of the opinion that the CPP is not a good investment. In their minds, paying into it is to be avoided if possible. Let's consider why they say this.

The first problem with coming to a definitive conclusion about whether the CPP is a good investment is that the analysis needs one key piece of information: how long are you going to live?

It would be quite easy to create a spreadsheet to come to a solid answer if we knew that. Take someone who elects to start receiving his CPP at age 65 and passes away at age 70. In hindsight, paying into the plan for 47 years from age 18 to 65 was a bad investment. If the person lived to 95, it would have been a great investment.

Unfortunately that is part of life—the number of years we'll collect our CPP pension is a wildcard. But that shouldn't stop us from trying to analyze our own CPP situation.

The first factor to consider is whether you are an employee or self-employed.

If you have a job, your employer is required to withhold CPP premiums from your pay, and contribute a matching amount to the government. If you are self-employed and operate as a sole-proprietorship or partnership, you report your net income (revenue less expenses) on your personal income tax return on line 135 ("Self-employment income—Net"). Your CPP premiums are calculated and the total is payable along with your federal and provincial or territorial tax on the last page of the return on line 421 ("CPP contributions payable on self-employment and other earnings"). You then get a tax deduction for half the CPP contributions on line 222 ("Deduction for CPP or QPP contributions on self-employment and other earnings"), and a non-refundable tax credit for the other half on line 310 of Schedule 1 ("CPP or QPP contributions: on self-employment and other earnings").

The key difference is that self-employed people are paying both portions of the CPP premiums since there is no other entity to cover half the cost. So for self-employed people the CPP costs twice as much as for employed people since you pay twice as much into it but get the same amount out at the end.

I have created a spreadsheet that you can download for free from my website at www.trahair.com. Just click on the title of this book on the left column and scroll to the bottom. Look for the Microsoft Excel file called "CPP Plan Rate of Return Calculator." The date it was last updated is at the end of the file name.

It is too large to reproduce in this book, but here are the assumptions I entered to illustrate the results for a sample person:

1. He turned 18 on January 1, 2000, and began paying into the CPP plan;
2. He earned more than the CPP Yearly Maximum Pensionable Earnings (YMPE) each year from age 18 (year 2000) to age 65 (year 2047);
3. He did not have any years of low income or child-rearing and therefore had no drop-out years;
4. He started his pension at age 65 on January 1, 2047;
5. CPP premiums and pension payouts were assumed to increase annually by the annual rate of inflation, assumed to be 2%.

The spreadsheet uses the Microsoft Excel formula for calculating the internal rate of return for a series of cash flows where cash outflows (CPP contributions in this case) are entered as negative numbers and cash inflows (CPP pension payments in this case). Here is what it looks like:

$$= XIRR(B1:B77,A1:A77)$$

The numbers representing the outflows and inflows would be listed in column B in this case and the corresponding dates of those inflows and outflows would be right next to them in column A.

In our example, the spreadsheet shows the internal rate of return to be 4.26% per year if he is employed all his life and only 2.21% if he was self-employed. This makes sense because he is paying double the amounts in as a self-employed person, for the same pension out.

What if I took out seven years for the drop-out provision at random over the 47 years of contributions? The internal rate of return for him as an employee rises to 4.68% and 2.69% if he was self-employed.

What if he unfortunately dies at age 78? Assuming no drop-out years, the internal rates of return are 3.11% and 0.72%.

I encourage you to download the spreadsheet and try to find out what your rate of return is rather than relying on this example. But assume your results indicate a similar internal rate of return—what does that mean?

Well, if you are employed all your life, what the internal rate of return is projected to be is irrelevant since you have to pay into the plan in any case.

The same is true if you are self-employed: you have to make payments to the CPP plan. And don't try to avoid that by reporting your self-employment earnings on the wrong line of your tax return. Some people try this—they report the earnings as "other income" not subject to CPP contributions. I have seen cases where CRA goes back many years—more than four—and assesses the taxpayer for both portions of the CPP premiums for each year. Add interest and penalties and that could be a huge amount.

I have also heard of people who have their own business structured as incorporated companies. The owners are paid as employees just like regular employees and have to remit CPP contributions, but the owners have an option. They could decide to stop taking a salary and remunerate themselves by taking only dividends. The people who do this argue there are certain tax advantages, and there may be, but I would not elect to do this for the following reasons:

- If you don't pay into the CPP, you will get nothing out of it at the end.
- If you don't pay into CPP, will you have the discipline to use those funds to invest in something else for your retirement?
- Even if you are disciplined, are you confident your investments will beat the rate of return that your CPP contributions and payouts would yield?
- If you need a mortgage or other loan it may be difficult to explain to a bank why you don't have a salary and therefore can't give them a copy of your T4 to prove your income.

Giving up a federal government-guaranteed defined benefit pension plan does not sound like a good idea to me. It could just be the number-one cash cow for you in your golden years.

How Is the Maximum CPP Pension Calculated?

The maximum CPP retirement pension for 2012 is $986.67 per month, which is $11,840 a year. How did that figure come to be?

It is equal to 25% of the average of the last five years' maximum pensionable earnings (YMPE). Here's how they got it.

Last five years' YMPE:

2008	$44,900
2009	$46,300
2010	$47,200
2011	$48,300
2012	$50,100
Average of the 2008 to 2012 YMPE (AMPE)	$47,360
25% of AMPE	$11,840
Monthly	($11,840/12) $986.67

CPP and QPP Maximum Amounts

The following table summarizes the maximum amounts of the CPP and QPP for 2012:[2]

Canada Pension Plan and Quebec Pension Plan – 2012		
Type of Benefit	**CPP**	**QPP**
Retirement (at age 65)	$986.67	$986.67
Disability	$1,185.50	$1,185.47
Survivor (younger than 65)	$543.82	See Note 1
Survivor (65 and older)	$592.00	$592.00
Children of disabled contributor	$224.62	$71.32
Children of deceased contributor	$224.62	$224.62
Death (maximum one-time payment)	$2,500.00	$2,500.00

Note 1: The maximum QPP disability benefit for a survivor between the ages of 45 and 64 is $815.47. For those younger than 45 it is $815.47

---

[2] http://www.servicecanada.gc.ca/eng/isp/statistics/rates/aprjun12.shtml

if disabled, $484.09 if not disabled with no child and $783.62 if not disabled, with child.

How Will My CPP Pension Be Calculated?

If you have worked every year from age 18 to 65 and earned more than the YMPE each of those years, you will have paid the maximum CPP premiums in your life. You would therefore receive the maximum retirement pension.

We have also seen that they give you a break for years where you earned less than the maximum (the general drop-out provision), which drops 16% of the years if you start in 2012 or 2013 and 17% of the years if you start in 2014.

According to Service Canada, when these years occur is irrelevant. In other words, it doesn't seem to matter whether you had low earnings when you were just starting your working years or nearing the end of them.

For most people the general drop-out provision is quite beneficial, because it recognizes that we all don't work and pay the maximum into the CPP every year from age 18.

This is especially useful for students attending university, who usually have low earnings years early—from age 18 to 22 or longer. This means that a person who began working at age 18 and always earned more than the YMPE and a student who graduated from university at age 23 and then started earning the maximum would both be eligible for the maximum CPP retirement pension even though the second student started paying into the CPP four years later.

There is also a helpful provision for those who haven't been able to pay into the CPP throughout their adult lives because they stayed home to raise children. It's called the child-rearing provision.

The Child-Rearing Provision

If you stopped work to be the primary caregiver for your children, or your earnings were lower while you raised your children under seven, you can request an exclusion of those years from the benefit calculation (the request is on the CPP retirement application form). This will ensure you get the highest possible payment because it ignores this low-earnings period in the calculation.

Note that for CPP purposes the primary caregiver is the person who was most responsible for the day-to-day needs of the children for the specified period. Either spouse or common-law partner can request the child-rearing provision, but both parents cannot use it for the same period of time.

It can only be used for months where:

- you or your spouse or common-law partner received Family Allowance payments or you were eligible for the Child Tax Benefit (even if you didn't receive it);
- your earnings were lower because you either stopped working or worked fewer hours to be the primary caregiver of a dependent child under seven who was born after 1958.

Note that you can only make one claim per year. In other words if you have more than one child under seven you don't get a higher provision.

If you are already receiving a CPP benefit and you did not request the child-rearing provision, Service Canada says you can contact them and they will check to see if you are eligible to request it.

The child-rearing provision could also help you meet the eligibility requirements for the CPP disability benefit, should you happen to need it, and in the event of your death could help you meet the contributory requirements to provide benefits to your estate and survivors.

To have this provision apply you must provide the original or a certified true copy of the child's birth certificate or the child's name, date of birth and Social Insurance Number. If the child was born outside of Canada, you may be required to provide proof of the date of entry into Canada.

It is interesting to note that Service Canada does this calculation first and then applies the general drop-out provision for low earnings years afterwards (i.e., 16% to 17% of remaining years). Let's look at an example.

Child-Rearing Provision Example

Let's say Judy had two children: Sammy, born in 2000, and Katy, born three years later in 2003. Judy can drop out 10 years for the child-rearing provision. That is the year 2000 when Sammy is born up to and including 2009 since Katy turned seven in 2010.

To be more precise, it's actually the number of months after Sammy is born until the month before Katy's seventh birthday.

Let's assume Judy plans to retire at 65 so we are dealing with a total contributory period of 47 years.

Of the 47 years, she can drop 10 for the child-rearing provision, which leaves 37 years. In 2012 under the general drop-out provision she can drop 16% of 37 years. That is six years (rounded), so she is left with 31 years for the calculation. If she contributed the maximum for those 31 years, she would be eligible for the maximum CPP retirement benefit.

Should I Elect to Start My CPP Early?

To do an accurate analysis you need to know your date of death. That poses a bit of a problem for most people. But the fact that we don't know how many years we are going to collect our CPP retirement benefit for does not mean it isn't worth thinking about. That is because the number of years we need to pay for after we retire will obviously have a large impact on the total cash inflows required to pay for it.

You may have heard a rule of thumb that says 83 is the magic age. If you think you will live longer than that, waiting until 65 to start your CPP pension is best. If your family history or other factors seem to indicate you won't live that long, electing early at age 60 would be the better option.

Unfortunately, it's not as simple as that. In fact, with the new rules regarding increased penalties for early election, it is very complicated to determine what is best.

But before we get into an analysis of the numbers, let's start with some basic questions.

Do You Need the Money?

First of all, ask yourself if you need the money. Say, for example, you are 60 years of age, retired from the workforce and have limited other financial resources. Go ahead and elect to start receiving your pension at age 60.

Will You Lose Money to Income Tax?

For those people who are still earning a good salary, who don't need the money, it makes less sense because the CPP retirement pension is taxable. Depending on where you live and your marginal tax rate you could lose a significant portion to income taxes. Here are the top marginal tax rates by province and territory for 2012 as of January 15, 2012:

B.C.	43.70%
Alberta	39.00%
Saskatchewan	44.00%
Manitoba	46.40%
Ontario	46.41%
Quebec	48.22%
N.B.	43.30%
N.S.	50.00%
P.E.I.	47.37%
Newfoundland	42.30%
N.W.T.	43.05%
Yukon	42.40%
Nunavut	40.50%

So if you received a CPP early pension of $1,000 in Alberta, the lowest-rate province, you would pay $390 in tax at the top bracket and only keep $610. In Nova Scotia, the highest-rate province, you would keep only $500 of every $1,000 you received.

Do You Have RRSP Contribution Room?

If you don't need the money and have room to make RRSP contributions, electing early may make sense. That is because you could effectively shelter the CPP retirement pension from tax. In other words, you receive the $1,000 in CPP pension, record it on your income tax return and then make a $1,000 contribution to your RRSP. You have essentially taken your CPP pension and invested 100% of it in your RRSP.

Remember, though, that an RRSP merely defers tax until you withdraw the funds later, but this strategy is much preferable to receiving the CPP amount and paying tax up front on it and only having the after-tax amount to invest over the coming years.

The strategy does not work for the TFSA option since contributions to your TFSA are not tax-deductible.

What Rate of Return Will Your RRSP Make?

The next question if you are considering doing this is: "How well do you think your RRSP investments will perform over the next five years?"

That is tough to answer, but you need to consider if the amount invested in your RRSP is likely to grow at a higher rate than the penalty for early election. Remember that the rate is going to increase from 0.52% per month (6.24%) in 2012 to 0.6% per month (7.2% per year) in 2016. A guaranteed rate of return above 6% a year is going to be very difficult to achieve consistently going forward. For this reason, it may make more sense to simply wait to collect your CPP pension until you need it.

Inflation Effect on the CPP Retirement Benefit

You also need to take into consideration the fact that once you start to receive the CPP retirement benefit, it is adjusted upwards for inflation each year as measured by the Total CPI.

The CPP pension is adjusted once a year using a 12-month moving average method, which helps smooth out fluctuations that may occur in one month. They use the average monthly Total CPI for the prior year's 12-month period ending in October. They use October because they need to publish the rates for the next year in the fall of the previous year.

The CPP Disability Benefits

Many people are not aware of the disability benefits provided for those who are paying into the CPP pension. It is another reason why I am a fan of paying into the CPP even if you have the option not to.

This section is important because even though the odds of meeting the stringent requirements are thankfully low, if a severe disability happens it is often a double whammy. You can't work to earn income, and the medical costs (yes, even in Canada) can become a cash pig. Many Canadians are under the impression that all medical expenses are covered, but a major illness shows them otherwise.

Here's what you need to know.

The CPP disability benefit is a monthly taxable benefit paid to contributors who have contributed to the CPP while they worked, and then became unable to work at any job on a regular basis because of a disability.

There are also benefits for children if at least one parent qualifies for the CPP disability benefit.

The disability has to be both "severe" and "prolonged," and must prevent you from working at any job on a regular basis. Even if you qualify for other government programs, or private program insurance, there is no guarantee that you will qualify for a CPP disability benefit. The CPP medical adjudicators make the decision based on your application and supporting documents.

The requirements to receive this benefit are quite stringent. A severe disability is defined as one that prevents you from doing any job, not just your former job, on a regular basis. Prolonged means that it is likely to be long term and of indefinite duration, or is likely to result in death.

If you qualify, it will stop if your condition improves to the point where you are able to work at any job on a regular basis, turn 65, or upon your death.

To be eligible you must have made enough CPP contributions in at least four of the last six years, or you must have made valid CPP contributions for at least 25 years, including three of the last six years, prior to becoming disabled. The basic exemption before you have to start contributing to the CPP for retirement benefits is $3,500, but for the disability benefits you need to have earned more than $4,800.

The benefit includes a fixed amount of $445.50 a month in 2012, plus an amount based on how much you contributed to the CPP during your entire working career. The most you can receive from the disability benefit each month in 2012 is $1,185.50.

Your dependent child under 18, or child between 18 and 25 who is attending school full time, can receive up to $224.62 a month in 2012 if you are approved for a disability benefit.

SUMMING UP THE CPP

The CPP pension is going to be an important component of most Canadians' retirement cash inflows, so it requires some analysis and consideration. We have seen that the plan is in solid shape and that we can therefore rely on it to be there when this cash pig turns into a cash cow.

But it is important that you give some thought to your own situation. How much are you likely to get, given the number of years and the amount you have paid into it? You also need to address the important issue of when to start to receive it—as early as age 60, but as late as age 70.

This chapter has given you the information and tools to determine what is best in your situation. The ball is now in your court. Resolve to think about your own CPP cash cow so you can rest easier on the journey to, and through, retirement.

CAN WE RELY ON THE OLD AGE SECURITY CASH COW?

The OAS pension is another aspect of your cash flow planning for retirement and therefore you need to be fully informed about what it is, how it works, and how it's going to change.

It is different than the CPP pension in that we don't make direct contributions to it during our working years. We become eligible to receive it simply based on our years living in Canada. That is a good thing—and also a bad thing, as we will soon find out.

The Old Age Security (OAS) program provides a modest monthly pension starting at age 65 if you have lived in Canada for at least 10 years. If you are a low-income senior, you may be eligible for other benefits, called an allowance, as early as age 60. You must apply for the OAS and also meet certain legal status and residence requirements. It is recommended that you apply six months before turning 65. You don't need to be retired and your employment history is not used to determine your eligibility.

THE OAS DETAILS

All OAS benefits are adjusted in January, April, July and October if there are increases in the cost of living as measured by the Consumer Price Index.

To qualify for an OAS pension, you must be 65 years of age or older, and must be a Canadian citizen or a legal resident of Canada on the day preceding your application's approval, or, if you are no longer living in Canada, you must have been a Canadian citizen or legal resident of Canada on the day preceding the day you stopped living in Canada.

A minimum of 10 years of residence in Canada after reaching the age of 18 is required to receive the pension in Canada and a minimum of 20 years is required if you are to receive your OAS pension outside of Canada.

The amount of your OAS pension is determined by how long you have lived in Canada as follows:

- If you have lived in Canada for 40 years after turning 18 you should qualify for a full OAS pension;
- If you have not lived in Canada for 40 years after turning 18 you may still qualify for a full OAS pension if, on July 1, 1977, you were 25 years of age or older; and
  - lived in Canada on July 1, 1977; or
  - had lived in Canada before July 1, 1977, after reaching age 18; or
  - possessed a valid immigration visa on July 1, 1977.

In the latter case, you must have lived in Canada for the 10 years immediately prior to approval of your OAS pension application.

Guaranteed Income Supplement

The Guaranteed Income Supplement (GIS) provides additional money on top of the OAS pension to low-income seniors living in Canada. The GIS also includes an allowance for persons whose spouse or common-law partner has died. It is an income-tested pension and thus eligibility and the amount of the payments will change depending on the reported income of the recipient and his or her spouse or common-law partner, if there is one.

To be eligible for the GIS benefit, you must be receiving the regular OAS pension.

The GIS is not taxable like the regular OAS pension and is not payable outside Canada beyond a period of six months after the date of departure, no matter how long the person has lived in Canada.

To start to receive the GIS, you only need to apply once and need not re-apply as long as you file an income tax return each year by April 30. If you do not file an income tax return, Service Canada will send you a renewal application form in the mail.

OAS Clawback

If your income exceeds certain amounts, you will have to pay back a portion or all of your OAS pension. In 2012, if your net income before adjustments (line 234 on your tax return) exceeds $69,562, called the "threshold amount," you will have to repay 15% of the amount by which your income exceeds the threshold.

For example, say your net income for 2012 was $85,000. You would have to pay back $2,315.70 ((85,000 − 69,562) × 15%).

The full OAS must be paid back when net income is $112,772 in 2012, since the net income above the threshold multiplied by 15% is $6,481.50, the maximum OAS pension for 2012 ((112,772 − 69,562) × 15%).

If you had to pay back a portion of your OAS pension this year, it will show as a deduction on line 235 of your tax return ("Social benefits repayment"). This is deducted from line 234 ("Net income before adjustments") to give line 236 ("Net income").

The amount is then added to the amount of tax you owe on the last page of your return on line 422 ("Social benefits repayment (amount from line 235)").

If you had to pay back any portion of your OAS pension, an appropriate amount will be deducted from the next year's OAS pension payments as a "Recovery Tax." For example, in the earlier example, $2,315.70 was paid back for 2012. The 2013 OAS recovery tax would be approximately $193 per month. When a recovery tax deduction is taken from your OAS pension payment, it is indicated in box 22 of your T4-OAS slip. You can claim that on the last page of your tax return on line 417 ("Income tax deducted"), just like you do for income tax on the T4 you receive for your employment earnings.

OAS AND GIS AMOUNTS

The following chart shows the maximum and average monthly amounts for OAS and GIS as well as the income level cut-off amounts for the period April to June 2012.[1]

Old Age Security Benefit Payment Amounts – April to June 2012			
Type of Benefit	Average Amount (January 2012)	Maximum Amount	Clawback
Old Age Security pension (OAS)	$510.21	$540.12	15% of net income above $69,562 Eliminated at net income $112,772 or above
Guaranteed Income Supplement (GIS)			Income level cut-off
Single	$492.26	$732.36	$16,368
Spouse of someone who does not receive OAS pension	$468.55	$732.36	$39,264
Spouse of someone who receives OAS pension	$309.28	$485.61	$21,648

Note that the maximum amount includes the new top-ups for the GIS effective July 1, 2011, and income level cut-offs do not include the OAS pension and the first $3,500 of employment income.

---

[1] http://www.servicecanada.gc.ca/eng/isp/oas/oasrates.shtml

The Proposed OAS Changes

The federal budget of March 29, 2012, proposed changes to the OAS program to make sure it remains healthy. The worry is that there is projected to be twice as many people aged 65 and over in 2030 as there were in 2011—9.4 million versus 5 million. Paying out OAS pensions to that many additional people would put significant pressure on the federal government's annual deficit because the OAS program is paid out of regular government revenue. In other words, it shows up as an expense on the federal government's annual statement of revenue and expenses.

Here are the changes proposed.

Age of Eligibility

The government proposes to increase the age of eligibility for the OAS and the GIS between the years 2023 and 2029, from age 65 to 67. This will affect you as follows:

If you were born in:

- **1957 or earlier.** If you were born in 1957 or earlier you will still be eligible for the OAS and GIS benefits at age 65.
- **1958.** If you were born before April 1, 1958, you will also not be affected by the proposed changes and will be eligible for the OAS and GIS benefits at age 65. If you were born in April or May you will have to wait one more month after turning 65. If your were born in June or July, it's two extra months. If you were born in August or September, it's three extra months and if you were born in October or November, it's four extra months. December births will have to wait five months after turning 65.
- **1959.** January births will have to wait five months after turning 65. February and March, six months. April and May, seven months. June and July, eight months. August and September, nine months. October and November, 10 months. December, 11 months.
- **1960.** January births will have to wait 11 months after turning 65. February and March births will have to wait until they turn 66. April and May, one month after turning 66. June and

July, two months after turning 66. August and September, three months after turning 66. October and November, four months after turning 66. December, five months after turning 66.

- **1961.** January births will have to wait five months after turning 66. February and March will have to wait six months after turning 66. April and May, seven months after turning 66. June and July, eight months after turning 66. August and September, nine months after turning 66. October and November, 10 months after turning 66. December, 11 months after turning 66.
- **1962.** January births will have to wait 11 months after turning 66. Anyone born after January will have to wait until they turn 67.
- **1963 or later.** Will have to wait until they turn 67.

Voluntary Deferral of OAS

The federal government proposes a voluntary deferral of the OAS pension for up to five years after the age of eligibility. If you elect to do this, you will receive a higher, actuarially adjusted pension when you do start to collect it. The pension will be increased by 0.6% per month of deferral, which is 7.2% per year.

It is proposed that the deferral option start in July 2013.

Proactive Enrolment for OAS Benefits

In a move that will benefit many seniors who are unfamiliar with the workings of the OAS and GIS pensions, the government proposes to start a proactive enrolment process that will reduce the risk that eligible seniors will not register for and therefore not receive pensions that they are entitled to.

Proactive enrolment is to be phased-in from 2013 to 2016, with eligible people to be notified by mail. Service Canada will continue to send applications to those seniors who cannot be proactively enrolled for OAS benefits.

The OAS applications form is also available for download from the Service Canada website at www.servicecanada.gc.ca. It is in Portable Document Format (PDF). The form is called "Application for the Old Age Security Pension" and includes a question asking if you'd like to apply for the GIS.

OAS WRAP-UP

The OAS pension is a small pension that plays a very important role for lower-income seniors and a lesser role for higher-income individuals since it gets clawed, or paid, back at higher levels of net income. It is also the subject of much scrutiny by the federal government because it is costing them more and more each year as the population ages. It is one of their cash pigs, and it's getting fatter by the day. That is why they are proposing to move the age of eligibility from 65 to 67.

But there is no doubt that to us, as individuals, the OAS pension is a cash cow if we receive it. The key is your situation in terms of eligibility and projected income levels. Don't plan on this cash cow unless you have considered all the issues we have addressed.

10

CASH FLOW
FOR LIFE

The key to setting yourself up for a comfortable retirement is to devote
some time to thinking about what your expenses are now and what
they are going to be in the future.

You can only do this if you take the time to track your current
expenses. Only then will you have the information to make a projec-
tion about what they are likely to be in the future. The vast majority
of people never bother to examine or summarize where their money is
going. That means a lot of personal financial planning is done "on the
back of a napkin," using easy and simplistic rules of thumb, which is
extremely dangerous.

For example, there is a rough rule of thumb that you'll need
approximately 70% of your pre-retirement earnings after you retire to
maintain your standard of living.

I made the case in my first book, *Smoke and Mirrors: Financial
Myths that Will Ruin Your Retirement Dreams,* that if you retire debt-
free with a paid-off home, you could get by on as little as 40% of your
pre-retirement earnings. That conclusion was based on a process I call
"Personal Financial Tracking." I used it for a sample family that I made
up using reasonable figures and assumptions about their incomes, tax
rates, housing purchase and maintenance costs, etc.

But it was all based on tracking the spending of the people involved.

Ever watched Gail Vaz-Oxlade's TV show called *Til Debt Do Us Part*? I love that show because it is based on detailed personal financial tracking. They always take the time to pore over the couple's spending before shocking them into reality. Just watch their faces as Gail tells them that they are spending $3,000 more than they bring home each month and that they'll be $300,000 further in consumer debt in five years if they continue their spending ways! Unfortunately, Gail can't visit everyone, so it's up to you to do this kind of tracking yourself.

Even if you don't go all-out using a software program such as Quicken from Intuit, at least get out your bank statements and credit card bills for the last month or more and total up what all the different categories are costing you. Many people are stunned at certain totals and this alone causes them to change their ways. After this exercise you should at least have some kind of idea about how much cash you will be spending each month and each year.

This can also be a motivating exercise for some people as they realize that some of their expenses will go away by the time they retire. Think about your monthly mortgage payment. Pay off your mortgage and you won't have that cash outflow each month after you retire. That usually makes a huge difference to the amount of cash needed during retirement.

WHAT ARE YOUR CASH COWS IN RETIREMENT?

One of the keys to a financially healthy retirement is to eliminate as many cash pigs as possible before you get there.

But since we also need to focus on maximizing our sources of income—our cash cows—let's review some of the basic sources of retirement income that could cover those expenses.

CPP and OAS

I have made the case that the CPP and OAS government pension plans are on solid ground and that we can count on them being there when we are retired.

The maximum CPP pension for 2012 is $986.67 per month ($11,840 annually).The maximum OAS pension as of June 2012 is $540.12 per month ($6,481.44 annually).

Remember that OAS begins to be clawed back at net income before adjustments of $69,562 and is totally clawed back at $112,772.

So the total combined maximum of CPP and OAS for 2012 is $1,526.79 per month ($18,321.48 annually). This is per person, so a couple that both worked and lived in Canada long enough to qualify for the maximum CPP and OAS pensions would be bringing in double that amount—$3,053.58 per month ($36,642.96 a year).

Your situation is probably different than that as you both may not have qualified for the maximums so obviously you need to project what your personal situation is, but I would say for most people that is a good basic guaranteed monthly pension amount.

CPP and OAS Death Warning

One thing that many people aren't aware of is the financially devastating effect of the death of a spouse when CPP and OAS are the main source of retirement funds.

When a person who is collecting CPP and OAS dies, Service Canada needs to be informed as soon as possible. They will then stop payment of the CPP and OAS pension to the deceased person.

The OAS is simply gone—that would be as much as $540.12 a month or $6,481.44 per year (as of June 2012) that would no longer be coming in.

The CPP survivor's benefit depends on the situation of the surviving spouse. If he or she had not been receiving a CPP pension because he or she did not pay any amount into the CPP, the maximum amount the survivor over age 65 would get in 2012 would be $592 a month, 60% of the $986.67 maximum the deceased was getting.

But there is a catch. Any one person can only receive up to the maximum retirement pension. If the surviving spouse is already getting the maximum, there is no additional amount paid to the survivor.

In this worst-case scenario of a couple in which each is earning maximum CPP and OAS, the survivor would lose $1,526.79 a month—that's $18,321.48 per year.

RRSPs: How Big Does Yours Need to Be?

If you have determined that the amount of income you'll need exceeds the total you are going to receive from CPP and OAS, you are going to need other sources of funds.

As we have discussed, it used to be common for this to be provided by employer-sponsored defined benefit (DB) plans. If you are one of the lucky ones to have worked for a company or government with a healthy DB pension that is adjusted for inflation, you may be set for life.

For the rest of us, a Registered Retirement Savings Plan is the most common answer. It needs to be large enough to provide the income to make up the difference between what you spend and what is covered by your CPP and OAS pensions.

Say, for example, you determine that you and your spouse will need $5,000 per month before tax in 2012 to live. Assume you each get $1,500 a month from CPP and OAS (a little less than the maximum) for $3,000 a month total. That means you'll need an RRSP to pay out $2,000 every month from retirement until your demise. That is $1,000 a month each.

The next issue is how long you'll need the money for. How long are you going to live?

Let's say you both will probably live to 85. That means each of your RRSPs at age 65 would need to be large enough to pay out $12,000 a year for 20 years.

Using a business calculator, a payment of $1,000 per month over 240 months (20 years), assuming the RRSP makes 5% per year, would mean an opening RRSP value of $152,156.

So your and your spouse's RRSPs combined would need to be worth a total of $304,312 at age 65.

But real life is a bit more complicated than this. How are you going to make a rate of return of 5% per year on your investments without taking undue risk? What happens if you have health concerns and need more than $5,000 a month?

Unfortunately, problems like these are more than likely to happen to you. The only way to ensure you are better able to deal with issues like this is to start getting your cash flow under control early in life. Leaving it until you are 75 years old is too late—you probably won't have the funds you'll need to live out your life in comfort.

Let's deal with the key issue when it comes to RRSPs, which is what happens when you turn 71.

Age 71: The End of Your RRSP

The year you turn 71 you have to convert your RRSP to a Registered Retirement Income Fund (RRIF) or an annuity. This is a vital decision as it will have a significant effect on the cash flow from your retirement savings going forward.

Registered Retirement Income Fund (RRIF) or Annuity?

An RRIF is simply your RRSP with a different name. You can transfer all the investments in your RRSP to your RRIF without triggering any tax so it's usually as simple as changing the name on your account. Once an RRIF is established there can be no more contributions made to the plan, nor can the plan be terminated except through death. You are allowed to take out as much as you want each year as there are no maximum withdrawal amounts. There are, however, minimum annual withdrawal amounts, depending on your age. We'll discuss those further below.

With an annuity, you purchase a contract from an insurance company with your RRSP funds and they guarantee to pay you a certain amount each month for life.

Let's explore the details of each.

RRIFs: The Details

The key thing to realize with RRIFs is that the government has minimum amounts that you must withdraw before December 31 of each year, depending on your age. If you have a younger spouse or a common-law partner, you can base it on his or her age. This would result in you having to take out less than if you used your age because the percentages increase with age.

Minimum RRIF Withdrawal Amounts

The minimum amounts are set by legislation and are expressed as a percentage of the opening market value of the RRIF account. If you establish an RRIF early, the percentage is 1/(90 – age). This applies up to age 70. So someone who is 70 would need to take out 5% (1/90 – 70).

Here are the percentages for RRIFs established after 1992 for age 69 and up:

RRIF Minimum Withdrawal Rates after 1992			
Age	%	Age	%
71	7.38%	83	9.58%
72	7.48%	84	9.93%
73	7.59%	85	10.33%
74	7.71%	86	10.79%
75	7.85%	87	11.33%
76	7.99%	88	11.96%
77	8.15%	89	12.71%
78	8.33%	90	13.62%
79	8.53%	91	14.73%
80	8.75%	92	16.12%
81	8.99%	93	17.92%
82	9.27%	94 or older	20.00%

With an RRIF you have flexibility. You can invest in a wide range of things, from fixed-income products such as GICs to stocks and mutual funds. You can also take out as much as you want each year, as long as it is above the minimum amounts.

But with this flexibility comes risk. What if you are over-exposed to equities and the stock market crashes again? What if you have a spending issue and end up taking out too much in the early years and don't have enough to last you to the end?

Purchasing an annuity with at least some of your RRSP might make sense.

Annuities: The Details

Annuities warrant consideration because they guarantee you cash flow for life after you buy them. You can't demolish your own finances by losing in the stock market because the insurance company has promised you cash flow for the rest of your life.

But let's review the basics.

Annuity Basics

An annuity is like the opposite of a mortgage. With a mortgage you borrow a large sum of money up front and make regular payments of principal and interest until the mortgage is paid off. With an annuity you make the big payment to an insurance company, and they make regular payments to you in return. The main difference is that a mortgage ends, whereas an annuity can be set up to pay an income for the rest of your life, or the rest of your spouse's life should you die first.

Single Life Annuity

As the name implies, a single life annuity is a contract provided by a life insurance company that pays a guaranteed income for a person's (the annuitant's) life. It is sometimes referred to as "straight life." The advantage is that you can't outlive your income. The disadvantage is that the money is locked in—it can't be recovered if you die soon after the annuity is purchased.

The insurance company takes into account your age, gender, marital status and health to determine how long they will likely have to pay you, which determines how much you will get each month.

Single life annuities pay more for males than females because mortality tables show that females have a greater life expectancy and therefore receive payments for longer.

Term-Certain Annuity

Term-certain annuities are paid for a fixed period and therefore you and the insurance company know how long the payments will be received by you, or your beneficiaries or estate if you die before the period ends.

For example, you could buy a life plus five-year annuity that would provide you with income for life but also guarantee 60 payments to your beneficiaries or estate if you die within the first five years.

This type of annuity will pay you less than a simple single life annuity because of the guarantee.

Indexed Annuity

This type of annuity will make payments for life that increase with inflation to maintain your purchasing power. This will cost more, meaning your starting payments will be lower than a single or straight life annuity.

Joint Annuity

A joint annuity pays a periodic income as long as one of the joint annuitants is alive. In other words, it provides income for life for you and your spouse because the payments only stop when both of you have died. It is sometimes referred to as a life plus joint-and-last-survivor annuity.

A joint annuity will be more expensive, or pay less per month, than a single life annuity because statistically the payments will go on for longer.

How Much Do Annuities Pay?

The amount they pay to you depends on many factors, including:

- **The amount of money you pay up front.** This is often called the premium. The higher it is, the higher your monthly payment will be.
- **Your age and gender.** Males receive higher payments due to the higher probability that they won't live as long as females.
- **Type of annuity.** If you add additional features such as a guarantee period, making it a joint annuity, or adding indexing, it will lower the monthly payments you receive.
- **Current interest rates.** The insurance company will invest your up-front premium since this is how they fund the payments. The higher interest rates and investment returns they can achieve, the higher your payments will be.

Current Annuity Rates

The current problem with annuities is that they don't pay very much compared to what they used to because interest rates are close to historical lows.

I just did a search for monthly annuity payments for a $100,000 life annuity. As of May 2012 the best rates I could find for a 65-year-old were:

- Male $498.77
- Female $452.11
- Joint $411.95

As you can see, females receive less for the same amount and joint policies pay even less.

What kind of rates of return are these providing? That depends on how long the payments go on for.

For example, assume the male lives until age 85. The effective annual interest rate on 20 years of payments (240 monthly payments) is about 1.87%.

If he lived until age 90, that rate would be 3.5% because he received more payments on his $100,000 premium. If he died at age 80 his effective rate of return would be 1.4%.

CASH FLOW FINALE

When you are entering your retirement years, expert personal financial planning advice becomes even more vital than it is during your younger years. That is because you don't have time to make up for bad decisions.

The decisions you make regarding your RRSP at age 71 are especially important.

You need a knowledgeable, qualified, independent advisor with insurance expertise to help you make the vital decision about whether to purchase an annuity with at least a portion of your nest egg. Many people don't even consider this option and go straight into an RRIF. With rising interest rates on the horizon, annuities may become an even more viable option in the years to come.

If you don't have a good advisor to help with these decisions, resolve to spend time trying to find one. I did and it was the best financial decision I ever made.

THE INHERITANCE
JACKPOT

There are supposedly billions of dollars waiting to be transferred to the baby-boom generation in the form of an inheritance.

You may even be one of them. If you are, you're probably wondering when and how much you'll get, right?

Obviously a healthy inheritance could be one of the biggest jackpots you'll ever see. Unfortunately, like most jackpots, an inheritance is not guaranteed. Most people can only guess at how much they'll get.

I first started thinking seriously about the transfer of wealth to the baby boomers in the summer of 2009. It was at the Word On The Street book festival in Toronto and I was there to speak about my book *Enough Bull*.

On stage before me was Patricia Lovett-Reid, who at the time worked at a financial institution and also had her own TV show on BNN. She now hosts a new show—*The Pattie Lovett-Reid Show* on CTV News Channel.

Pattie told the story of a woman she met who had been married to a wealthy business owner. The couple had a $2 million life insurance policy on the husband's life. This was a good move because he sadly got very sick and passed away in a short period of time.

Unfortunately, the life insurance policy payments had not been renewed just one month prior to the husband's death. You can understand that happening during such an emotionally devastating period of time; opening and reading the mail would not have been top of mind for this woman.

What do you think happened?

The life insurance company would not budge. They declined to pay the $2 million tax-free death benefit. The woman had to take the insurance company to court and eventually settled—for $75,000.

The lack of attention to an administrative detail cost her $1.925 million.

Pattie's story is just one of many. Here's another.

I was teaching a class of CAs and one CA told me the story of a husband and wife who were his clients. They had literally buried $50,000 worth of gold bullion in the ground near their favourite camp site. "Does anyone besides you and your wife know where it is?" he once asked the guy. "No," was the response. "What if you both die in a car accident?" The response was "Oh, that won't happen..."

After thinking about it for a few days, a map to the gold was drawn up and placed with the client's will.

THE GREAT WEALTH TRANSFER IS GOING TO BE INEFFICIENT

It is stories such as these that make me believe the great transfer of wealth between the generations is going to be a very inefficient process. In many cases, the person who is supposed to receive the inheritance is going to lose out.

In some instances, like the buried gold case, it's possible that no one will win. The wealth could be lost forever.

In other cases, like the lapsed life insurance case, a lot of the wealth will get "absorbed" by the big financial institutions. This would also include things such as bank and investment accounts that are forgotten about.

Here's why I believe that millions of dollars are going to be lost:

- **Human nature.** Most people don't relish the thought of poring over paperwork after a hard day at the office. Many people live their lives without paying much attention to their personal finances. This is unlikely to change, especially as they age. As a result, key documents will be lost.

- **Death is depressing.** Put yourself in the shoes of the previous generation—your parents. Would you want to talk about your imminent demise? Of course not. No one likes to plan for their own funeral. That makes it difficult to discuss.
- **Aging is bad for the memory.** Unfortunately, getting old sucks. Our bodies start letting us down and, in many cases, so do our minds. We start forgetting things. And that will mean a lot of wealth that should pass on will not.

Combine the lack of organized paperwork and records, a depressing subject and people starting to forget things, and you have a recipe for wealth transfer mayhem.

How to Talk to Your Parents About Death

Talking about death with your parents is probably going to be one of the toughest things you'll have to do. It can sound very selfish; after all, you have a conflict of interest as you'll (hopefully) be the recipient when your parents eventually pass away.

Of course even if you take the time and effort to discuss things, there may not even be much of an inheritance. Many people are living longer, and in many cases are incurring the high cost of retirement and nursing homes.

Here are a few ideas to help you broach the subject of inheritance to encourage your parents to start planning sooner, rather than leaving it all until after they are gone.

- **Mention the grandkids.** If you have kids, bring up the idea that you could use any financial assistance they would be willing to offer to help raise their grandchildren.
- **Bring up the issue of their own medical care.** If you don't know where your parents' money is and they need medical and other care but are not capable of taking care of their own finances, the money will come from your pocket. That doesn't make much sense.

The Problem with Death

When death comes it is often a surprise. It's also, obviously, an extremely emotional period of time and taking care of the finances is the last thing most people want to think about.

The most important thing you can do is prepare for its eventuality as best you can. Then, when it happens, at least you won't have to worry about basic stuff like where your parents keep their will or insurance documents.

IS THERE TAX ON DEATH?

In Canada there is no formal death or inheritance tax that beneficiaries have to pay on receiving an inheritance.

What does happen on death is that the deceased is deemed to have disposed of all his or her assets immediately prior to death. The final tax return of the deceased covers the period from January 1 to the date of death. Tax is therefore owing on such things as capital gains on any stock investments held outside a TFSA. The final balance on the person's RRSP or RRIF will also be fully taxable unless there is a surviving spouse or common-law partner, in which case the balance can be transferred to him or her on a tax-free basis.

There may, however, be an estate administration tax, often referred to as probate fees depending on the province or territory where you live, but this is not a formal inheritance tax.

The taxation issues involved in a larger estate can become exceedingly complex. It is best that you consult a professional estate administrator and tax specialist to ensure that the taxation and other issues are handled correctly.

GETTING READY: A SIMPLE CHECKLIST

The following is a short list of questions to help ensure that the transfer of wealth in your case goes as smoothly as possible. It is for general information only. You should contact an experienced lawyer to make sure that your specific situation is handled properly.

- Do you have a will?
  - Where is the latest copy of the will? (law firm name and address)

- List of all bank accounts, including:
  - Bank name, branch, mailing address, account numbers
  - Approximate balance in each account
- List of all RRSP accounts, including:
  - Broker/discount broker name, mailing address, account numbers
  - Approximate balance in each account
- List of all RRIF accounts, including:
  - Broker/discount broker name, mailing address, account numbers
  - Approximate balance in each account
- List of all investment and TFSA accounts, including:
  - Broker/discount broker name, mailing address, account numbers
  - Adjusted cost base of each investment outside a TFSA
- List of any debts, including:
  - Mortgage, line of credit or reverse mortgage on the principal residence
  - Unsecured lines of credit
  - Other debts
- List of all credit cards, including:
  - Bank or institution name, mailing address, account numbers
  - Credit limits and approximate balance
- Copy of last three year's income tax returns and CRA assessments

This checklist is just a basic list to get you started. Estate planning is emotional, complicated and very important. It is for these reasons that you should get professionals involved as follows:

- **Lawyer.** For wills, probate issues, Power of Attorney, trusts, etc.
- **Financial planner or investment advisor.** For investment management and transfer.
- **Insurance specialist.** For life insurance and other insurance issues.
- **Accountant.** For income tax planning and compliance.

I hope I have given you some of the basic information to spur you to take control of the estate planning issue within your family. Encourage your parents to talk about it. Don't ignore this vital part of life.

CONCLUSION

I have made the case throughout this book that the key to a healthy and fulfilling life is not to aim to become "rich" but to simply make sure your cash inflows match your cash outflows during your working and retirement years.

During your working years, that means you have to control your spending so that you spend less than your after-tax income or your take-home pay. This is the hard part. It is even hard for most people to determine if they even are spending more than they make.

In the old days, when credit cards and debt instruments such as lines of credit were not so freely available, people's spending was automatically controlled. You could not physically spend more than you had in your bank account. That is not the case today. There are many people who spend much more than they earn each year—by running up their credit cards and lines of credit. If you are one of them, and can't pay off your credit card and have a line of credit that goes nowhere but up, take a deep breath and resolve to change your habits. If you don't, you are on the way to almost certain personal financial disaster, sooner or later.

You need to take control and live life within your means during your working years to give yourself a chance of contentment during your retirement years. If you are already retired, the best time to start taking control of your cash inflows and outflows was in the past. The second best time is today.

INDEX

ABOUT THE AUTHOR

David Trahair is a Chartered Accountant who operates as a sole-proprietor, offering a broad range of accounting and tax services to a variety of businesses and individuals. He belongs to the Canadian Institute of Chartered Accountants and the Institute of Chartered Accountants of Ontario. He is a frequent speaker, appears regularly in the media, contributes regularly to financial publications, and is the author of several books, including *Enough Bull* and *Crushing Debt*. He is also a previous director of Credit Canada, a non-profit organization dedicated to helping people deal with credit problems, for six years.